the man who made Milwaukee famous

a salute to Henry Aaron

the man who made Milwaukee famous

a salute to Henry Aaron

by *Don Money*
with
Herb Anastor

agape publishers, inc.
MILWAUKEE, WISCONSIN

Publisher	Robert C. Dougherty
Editorial Director	Mike Kupper
Production Director	David R. Dumke
Production Associate	Kathy Malczewski
Jacket Design	Bob Berendsen
Special Photography	Ernest W. Anheuser
Color Preparation	American Color Systems
Lithography	Sells Printing
Typography	A-Line Typographers
Line Art	Jeff Hargreaves

The Man Who Made Milwaukee Famous —
A Salute to Henry Aaron

Library of Congress Catalog Card Number: 76-1812

ISBN: 0-914618-03-2

All rights reserved.

Published by Agape Publishers, Inc.
10721 West Capitol Drive, Milwaukee, Wisconsin 53222

Printed in the United States of America

First Printing: April 1976

The Man Who Made Milwaukee Famous

the man who made Milwaukee famous

a salute to Henry Aaron

Contents

To my wife, Sharon —
and our children,
Donald and Shannon

Introduction

Without a doubt, Hank Aaron has become one of the most legendary characters to ever play the game of baseball. By the breaking of Babe Ruth's home run record in April, 1974, he insured his place in baseball history. But there is much more to Henry Aaron than just his skill with a bat. There is the human side to the man, which — for the most part — has been explored and reported only from a distance by writers and biographers. They are able to enter only briefly, then exit the closed quarters of the baseball world to gather their information and impressions.

My intention here is to present a picture of Hank Aaron as he is seen by a fellow ballplayer, a teammate. My position as a member of the Milwaukee Brewers puts me in close contact with him. It also allows me to observe closely a man ending his years of professional baseball, and to see how he accepts the end of a brilliant career, how he is received by the fans who got to know him more than twenty seasons ago, and how he is welcomed and honored by the fans of the American League who have had little opportunity to see one of baseball's finest representatives as an everyday player.

What follows is something I hope will be looked upon as a true picture of Hank Aaron, the man and athlete. My only hope is that in years to come, those who have known Henry Aaron — and even the man himself — will look favorably upon what is written here and say, "Yes. It truly was that way."

Don Money

19

Chapter 1

We've Got
The Hammer

Hank Aaron is my teammate. That may have little significance, but the events before and after he left the Atlanta Braves and joined the Milwaukee Brewers certainly do.

It was somewhere around the middle of October, 1974, when I first heard of the possibility of our getting Aaron for 1975, and maybe beyond. I never dreamed of it until I started seeing articles in the papers saying that Aaron wanted to play at least one more year, but that he didn't want to play that year in Atlanta. He wanted to come back to Milwaukee, according to the stories.

A lot of people probably wondered why Hank wanted to keep on playing ball. By breaking Babe Ruth's career record of 714 home runs, he had already earned a special niche in the Hall of Fame. But from what I knew about the man as an opponent, I could understand why he wanted to play at least one more year before he hung up his spikes for good.

When you get down to it, 1974 was not a typical year for Hank Aaron. Sure, he hit twenty home runs and broke the record, but that was just about all that there was to the season for him. The Braves finished fourteen games behind the Los Angeles Dodgers in third place in the National League West, and weren't really in the pennant race during much of the year. Henry's batting average with the Braves in 1974 was only .268 — another reason why he might want to play another year or two, get the old average back up around .300, then call it a career at the top.

There was a lot of talk during the World Series that some announcement would be forthcoming about where Hank was going to play in 1975, if indeed he was going to play another year. Nothing really came of all the speculation until November 2. Henry was on a goodwill tour in Japan, where he was scheduled to have a home run hitting contest with the top slugger in Japanese baseball, Sadaharu Oh. The contest was shown on a taped delay that Saturday over the CBS television network. After Henry had defeated Oh, he was asked what his plans were for 1975. Hank said that he expected some announcement to be made soon, but there was nothing he could say at the time.

What all of us watching didn't know was that the "soon" Hank was talking about would be the very next day. As Hank and Oh pumped baseballs out of an Oriental ball park, Bill Bartholomay, board chairman of the Atlanta Braves, and Bud Selig, president of the Brewers, completed a deal that brought Hank Aaron back to the city where he broke into major league baseball, the city that never forgot him.

The papers were full of Hank Aaron stories for the next couple of days. I can remember reading how happy Hank was to be sent back to Milwaukee and that he was pleased that the Braves had honored his request to be traded to the Brewers. Reports were that Hank had planned to retire after the 1974 campaign, but that when he was given the opportunity to come back to Milwaukee as a designated hitter, he immediately changed his mind.

That, of course, was just a great idea in the minds of most Milwaukee fans, who have been appreciating, and marveling at, Hank's skills since he was a skinny rookie with the Milwaukee Braves in 1954.

I don't remember it, since I was only 10 at the time and living out East, but they tell me Hank turned the town absolutely upside down with one of his homers. It was the night of September 23, 1957, and the Braves needed one more victory to clinch the National League pennant for the first time since the team's move from Boston in 1953.

The St. Louis Cardinals were in town, and for the longest time it looked as though they were going to deny the Braves that clinching victory. Hank took care of things, though. With two out, the score tied at 2-2 and Johnny Logan on first in the last of the 11th, Hank hit the first pitch Billy Muffet threw to him 400 feet over the center field fence.

Instant bedlam, not only at the stadium, where the crowd went wild, but downtown as well. At 11:30, four minutes before Hank's shot gave the Braves their 4-2 victory, Wisconsin Avenue, Milwaukee's main street, was practically deserted. At 11:35, it sprang to life in an impromptu celebration that continued until nearly 4 in the morning.

Thousands of people suddenly materialized out of restaurants and taverns, and more joined the growing throng from other parts of town by the minute. The happy crowd finally grew so great that the street had to be closed to motor traffic. The Braves had won the pennant and Milwaukee was in the mood to celebrate.

As it turned out, there was an even bigger celebration a couple of weeks later, when the Braves beat the Yankees in the World Series, but it didn't quite match that first one for sheer spontaneity, I'm told.

And there was no doubt who was the toast of the town. Hank Aaron, with that home run — the 109th of the 745 he had hit going into the 1976 season — stamped himself for all time as one of Milwaukee's own.

There have been others who have brought fame and glory to Milwaukee. Actors Pat O'Brien and Spencer Tracy once called Milwaukee home. The singer who bills herself as The Incomparable Hildegarde is from Milwaukee. Bandleader Woody Herman, he of the many Herds, learned to play the clarinet when he was growing up in Milwaukee. And there have been other athletic stars — Warren Spahn, Don Kojis, Kareem Abdul-Jabbar, to name just a few.

To the serious and dedicated baseball fan, though, there is no question about it. It's Hank Aaron, the man who made Milwaukee famous.

I first got some idea what Hank Aaron meant to the fans of Milwaukee in 1973, my first year with the Brewers. We were playing a midseason exhibition game with the Braves at County Stadium, and the occasion had been dubbed "Hank Aaron Night."

By the time the game was played, it was pretty obvious that Henry was going to break Babe Ruth's record, maybe even before that season was over. As it turned out, he fell two short in '73, but even if the fans had known that, I don't think it would have made any difference. The people of Milwaukee were way ahead of the rest of the fans around the country when it came to Hank's assault on the record. He was their champion, and champions just don't let you down. They had learned that in the 12 seasons Hank had spent with the Braves in Milwaukee.

Milwaukee really responded to "Hank Aaron

Night" and about 35,000 fans turned out to see their longtime hero. It was an experience for me to see and hear them express their admiration and love for this man. The ovations he received when he stepped to the plate or took his position in the field were just tremendous. He had been gone from the constant view of the Milwaukee fans for seven years, but obviously he had not been forgotten.

Everyone in the park that night was there to honor Henry, but the crowd also wanted to see him hit one out. A homer in an exhibition game would have no bearing on his run for the record, but it was all part of the expectant atmosphere. I believe even the players were anxious to see it. Billy Parsons was on the mound for us when Henry did it. As soon as Hank made contact with Billy's pitch, everyone in County Stadium knew it was gone. The place just exploded with another rousing tribute to the man. Later, my wife Sharon told me that many of the people in the stands had tears running down their faces as Aaron rounded the bases.

I didn't get my first chance to see Hank in action until the 1969 season, when I was with the Philadelphia Phillies and he was still with the Braves. That was my first full year in the bigs, but it was Henry's 16th, so I can't tell you first hand just how good a player he was in his prime.

I'll tell you one thing, though. It was a big thrill for me to just see him for the first time. In 1969, most of the spotlight was on the possibility that Willie Mays would break Babe Ruth's home run record. Hank Aaron was still out of the picture in the minds of many. But as I watched him take batting practice, I could hardly believe what I was seeing. There, right in front of me, was a man I'd read about in books, newspapers and magazines, doing what he did best. And I was lucky enough to have a front row seat. I think the same feeling came over me the first time I saw Mays and Al Kaline, Frank and Brooks Robinson, and all the rest of the truly great stars in the game. Each time was an experience I'll never forget.

What impressed me most at the time was Henry's friendliness. When I'd get to first, if he was playing there, or when he'd be on second — my first year in the majors was at short — I found him not at all reluctant to talk between pitches with an eager rookie. As a competitor against him, I really enjoyed playing the games we had with the Braves.

Now that I have spent a season with him, I know that my first impressions of him were true ones. In spring training — my first occasion to be with him for more than a brief time — I was as uneasy about approaching him as the next man. But as the season went on, it became very easy to talk with him and develop a relationship that felt warm and comfortable.

Sitting on the bench with him — and what with my being out of action for a third of the year with a hernia operation and a groin pull, I had a lot of time to do that — and talking about different things, I found him to be a real fine man, not at all hard to know. We talked about the various pitchers and hitting, but we also chewed the fat about hunting and fishing, and even some things that were far removed from baseball and the sporting world. Heck, to tell the truth, I think we got along great!

The success that Aaron has had over the years doesn't seem to have tainted his outlook on who he is and where he is going. He may be the man who made Milwaukee famous, but he will never tell you that.

Still, it's tough to write about Hank Aaron, or even think about him, and shut out the thought that he is the greatest home run hitter of all time. Even months after he hit homer No. 715, I was still being questioned by friends and fans about Henry's remarkable record.

That early April evening in 1974 is something I'll always remember. Like millions of others, I saw the historic shot go out of Atlanta's ball park on TV. The date, April 8, was an off-night for most ball clubs. We had just flown into Cleveland from Milwaukee for our first trip of the year, after splitting a pair with the Boston Red Sox at home.

With not much to do in the hotel, with the Braves-Dodgers game on the tube, and with Aaron having tied the record just four days earlier, most of us wanted to watch. We were all kind of hoping he might hit number 715 for the television audience.

I'm not sure whether it was because we were ballplayers or not, but there was a definite air of expectation every time Henry got up to bat. We had to wait only four innings before what we all knew would happen finally did.

With no outs and Darrell Evans on first, Hank came up with the Braves behind, 3-1. The Dodgers had Al Downing on the mound and his first pitch was a ball. On TV, Downing's next pitch looked like a pretty good fast ball. But when the man at the plate took his cut, he connected with the kind of swing that tells you the ball is going nowhere but out. Suddenly the score was tied at 3-3 and Henry Aaron had become the greatest home run hitter in the history of the game.

The television cameras showed the ball being retrieved by the Atlanta bull pen members. During the instant replay, while the commentators for NBC-TV were expounding on the shot, I couldn't help but notice the way Hank accepted his place in baseball history. As he was shown rounding the bases, my thoughts went back to the times I had seen his home run trot while I was with the Phillies. There was no difference. He circled the Atlanta infield on the night he made history the same way he had done it when I was a member of the opposition. Hank made his way around the bases deliberately, without showmanship. He went into the record book with the same style and class he had exhibited throughout his career. That meant something to me.

Chapter 2

"Hey, Don! How Ya Doin'?"

Off-seasons usually go pretty fast for me. I keep busy around my farm at home, go on a couple of hunting trips and do basketball play-by-play on my home-town radio station. But I don't think anything came up on me as fast as the month of January, 1975.

On January 13, I flew out of Philadelphia to Milwaukee for a 15 day stay. My primary reason for going was to help with publicity for the coming season, but I was also going to get my contract straightened away and to attend the Milwaukee baseball writers' dinner at the end of the month. A sidelight, but one that I was looking forward to, was the chance to renew acquaintances with our newest team member, Hank Aaron.

The publicity side of my trip took me to about a dozen luncheons and dinners in and around the Milwaukee area. It was my job to meet the people, answer questions and give the fans some idea of what to expect from the 1975 Brewers. I'd go to these meetings with either Dick Hackett, our ticket manager, or with his assistant, Steve Comte. They'd be the ones to get me where I was supposed to be and also sign up people for season tickets or make arrangements for community nights. Community nights in Milwaukee County Stadium are nights when a large group of fans from an outlying smaller city come to the park, get their name on the scoreboard and are saluted by the club prior to the start of the game. It's something most clubs do to get suburban and rural fans out to the ball park.

The vast majority of questions put to me by the fans were those concerning Hank Aaron and what his acquisition was going to mean to the club.

For many of the fans, Henry's return to their city was the return of major league baseball to the State of Wisconsin. Some of the real old-timers were sort of resentful toward the Brewers when they came to town, so I am told. They were still bitter because the Milwaukee Braves had vacated the city for Atlanta after so many good years in town. Some sports fans are like that. They'll hang onto a player or a team, no matter what the fortunes of the personality or group might be, because they believe there is something about the man or organization that is worth hanging onto. From what I could see at the functions I attended, there were many dyed-in-the-wool Hank Aaron fans who would be coming back to the ball park just to see him again.

But, there were lots at those luncheons and dinners who couldn't have remembered Aaron playing in Milwaukee at all. Kids would come up to me after the program was over and ask just about the same questions concerning Aaron that had been put to me only minutes before. You could see by the way these young fans asked the questions again that they just wanted a little reassuring that Hank Aaron was indeed coming to play for "their town."

Besides those appearances, the Brewers also arranged for me to spend some time on the radio and TV. The radio shows were the kind that allowed fans to call and ask questions or make comments. With the exception of a few questions about my career, most of the inquiries were about Hank Aaron and what kind of a guy he was. He had definitely made an impact.

My first meeting with Hank Aaron as a teammate really didn't last more than a few minutes. I had just walked down the hall in the Brewers' offices when he walked in. He didn't recognize me and I didn't say anything to him. But after a few minutes, he came out of Bud Selig's office, recognized me, walked over and said casually, "Hey, Don. How ya doin'?"

He apologized for not recognizing me at first, and we walked down to the ticket office together, small-talking about the off-season, how our families were and things like that.

Our second meeting, a week later, was not much different. It was late in the afternoon, and Hank and I were down in the office passing time with Bud Selig and some of the others in the front office. Mr. Selig wanted to show Henry the new construction going on out in the stadium.

We talked about which way the wind usually blows and how the new seats in left field might effect it, but I didn't notice any nostalgic reaction as Hank walked about the grounds that he had for so long called home. I can imagine, though, that even as we stood shivering in the depths of winter, Henry was reflecting on the good memories he had from his years in Milwaukee with the Braves — memories that are fond and warm and deeply satisfying, but belonging to a man whose very nature does not allow him to say, "Well, when I was here back in '57 I did so and so."

I guess the longest time I spoke with Henry while we were in Milwaukee that winter was at the baseball writers' Diamond Dinner at the Pfister Hotel. Before the start of the banquet, there was a cocktail party. Of course, Henry was the center of attention.

There were about 900 at the Diamond Dinner, and when Henry arrived at the dais, the fans greeted him with a standing ovation. The welcome Hank got was enough to give anyone there a good case of goose pimples. Aaron had said many times that his return to Milwaukee meant that he was coming back to the major leagues, and it was evident by the reception that he was more than welcome back home.

After the meal, those of us at the head table were honored. Besides Aaron, who received an achievement award for his excellent years of major league play, the group included Ferguson Jenkins of the Texas Rangers, Ken Holtzman of the Oakland A's, John Hiller of the Detroit Tigers and Brewers Tom Murphy, Robin Yount, George Scott and myself.

Fergie Jenkins got the Come-back Player of the Year Award for 1974 and Holtzman was recognized for his performances in the World Series of recent years. John Hiller got the Courageous Heart Award for his return to baseball as a winning pitcher for the Tigers after suffering a heart attack a couple of seasons back.

The award that Tom Murphy got from the writers was for his pitching performances of 1974 as he came on strong at the end of the season to be our best guy on the mound. Robin Yount was the recipient of the Rookie of the Year Award. Scotty got the Magic Glove Award from the writers to mark the fact that he was the best fielding first baseman in the league. I got a Magic Glove for my play at third and was also honored as the Most Valuable Brewer of 1974.

We all got up to say a few words of thanks, but when Hank got up, he did more than say thanks. With the spotlight of the entire evening centered on him, he thanked the writers for his award and then commented about the rest of us who had been honored that night. It was a great feeling to be sitting up on the dais with Aaron and hearing him talk about me in words that you figure are only for guys classed as big time stars. It was hard not to be embarrassed. What Aaron said about me, and being honored by the people I play in front of most of the year, meant more to me than some of those national honors and awards a player can get if he is known well enough to a national audience or media group. I think that each one of us will never forget Henry's tributes to us.

I know that I was a little surprised to learn during Henry's talk that the Atlanta Braves wanted to trade for me in 1972 and that they asked Aaron to put in a scouting report on me. But then when he said that I was the only player that he had ever been asked to scout, I just couldn't believe it. That alone taught me something that I had thought about before, but that was now more deeply impressed within me. You can never tell who is watching you when you are out on the field, or who might give you a compliment.

Afterward, while the rest of us were just mingling, Hank was surrounded by well-wishers and autograph seekers. After what had been a hectic day, Henry still found time to serve those who sought his attention.

Hank had many requests for appearances to fill during his days in town. One such session involved him and me posing with some Easter Seal young-sters at the stadium. Hank was only supposed to be there for a few minutes, but he stayed lots longer, giv-ing each child some of his attention. And then, to top it off, he thanked them for coming out to the park. That, to me, showed the kind of class Hank Aaron has.

Chapter 3

It Starts in the Spring

Spring training doesn't really start in the spring, but in the lingering months of an often all-too-long winter. In baseball, "spring" may arrive anytime from the end of February to the first days of March. And it may arrive for the pitchers and catchers anywhere from ten days to two weeks earlier than for the rest of the team. When spring training does start, it is for many players the beginning of a kind of vacation from the hectic weeks of the off-season — a five month period of baseball inactivity filled with things from home repairs to business dealings.

For the 1975 Milwaukee Brewers, spring began on Sunday, March 2, the reporting date to our training site in Sun City, Arizona. Although we would not be doing any actual work until the following day, the atmosphere around this well-known retirement community almost immediately turned to baseball. The residential base for most of us was at the 100 West Motel, a short walk from the stadium, and it wasn't long before that old feeling of being on the road came back to mind. Guys found their roommates — Timmy Johnson and I were together for another year — or joined others in the lobby, talking of off-season activities and the delight of being back in summery weather. The leisurely atmosphere was a welcome experience. We knew that in less than twenty-four hours we would be back to getting in shape for the baseball season.

For the veterans who have a secure job with the club, spring training is a time to work out the kinks and resharpen the skills. For young players just coming up, it's a time to show the brass how much improvement has been made, with an eye set on impressing enough to become a member of the big club when it finally travels north. That happened to Robin Yount in 1974, and it can happen every spring.

For some, spring is also a time for guys to show management how much they have developed after a winter of playing in the Caribbean. Winter ball is a good place to work on skills or try to learn something new that will help further a playing career.

Spring is also a time when a player may find that his job has been taken by a younger guy, or even that he is no longer a valuable item on the player market. Just as careers are started in camp, some also are ended — or delayed a bit as players get reassigned to the minor leagues. All of these are part of the game, and part of spring training.

Whatever the individual cases, though, the situation in Sun City was to start getting ready as a team. And as a team we would all be getting to know Henry Aaron.

For the first few days of training, we all were pretty impressed simply to be aware that Hank Aaron would be our teammate. The younger players felt his presence even more deeply than most of the veterans. Some of them hadn't even been born when Henry came to bat in the big leagues for the first time. For many of the younger guys, it was like having a bubble gum card come to life!

But this awe of Aaron was not reserved just for the younger guys. I know that I was struck by his appearance the first time I saw him in a Brewer uniform. I just couldn't stop thinking that the man wearing Number 44 was the greatest home run hitter in the history of baseball. That feeling filtered through the entire club.

It's hard to grasp the fact that the individual you are seeing is in fact the person whose name and likeness are so familiar. Seeing Aaron on the field those first couple of days took a little getting used to.

There was also a reluctance on the part of some of the younger players to go up to Henry and talk with him. That was natural, but it wore away quickly as training progressed. Even though I had played against Aaron in the National League and had been with him in Milwaukee only a few weeks before, I still was a little shy. Most of us kept our distance for the first couple of days because we didn't want to over-react to his membership on the club, but also because he was constantly being asked by people to take pictures with them or to sign just one more program or ball. In Henry's case, that just-one-more situation could last for hours. We kept respectfully away from him to give him a little breathing room and to allow him to get to know us at a more comfort-able pace.

Henry helped ease the situation himself when he started to join in the conversations around the batting cage. The first thing he asked me about was if any of the guys played golf. Not long afterward, an after-noon on the links was planned and a whole gang of us went out and played. Skill on the job really has nothing to do with skill on the golf course, even among professional athletes. So we went out as a team to have a good time, and Hank Aaron just wanted to be included as one of the guys.

The ice was broken with the veterans at first. Henry had gotten to know most of us, either by playing against us or by being in a situation where it was necessary to have some kind of friendly relationship going. As he got to know more of the guys, you could see that any respect barrier was turning into the formation of a teammate relationship. Aaron's friendliness let everyone know that he was interested in being treated as a member of the Milwaukee Brewers, and not someone over and above the rest of us. That attitude had a lot to do with the easy feeling that developed among the players toward Henry Aaron.

There certainly was no open resentment toward Aaron by the veterans, even though it was a sure thing that the No. 1 attraction for us now was most definitely the new guy. There might have been some deep-down feelings about his taking the limelight away, but nobody ever mentioned it.

Even George Scott, our resident slugger and the guy who was hurt most in the publicity department, said that Hank was the only guy he would ever even consider playing second fiddle to. In fact, he took his "lesser" role very optimistically. Boomer felt that by hitting behind Aaron, he would get better pitches and less pressure. George came to camp $750 overweight, but he had always been one of the hardest workers in the spring and, like the rest of us, was aware that we had to get ready to face a 162 game schedule. Worrying about who is going to be the top man at the end of the year doesn't get the job done. Anyone who had the idea that having Hank on the club would cause dissension was sadly mistaken. About the only problems we could see Aaron causing were for opposing pitchers.

One of the things that impressed me about Hank

Aaron's first spring as a Milwaukee Brewer was the way he dealt with the almost endless requests for his time by the fans. For many of them, this was the first time they had seen the man in person.

Hank handled their requests like a real pro and gentleman. Mostly, those who asked for autographs were fans who wanted to wish him good luck and have the thrill of meeting a sports legend. They were respectful in their approach to Hank and he returned the courtesy. If he was waiting his turn in the batting cage and was asked to come over for a picture or autograph, Hank would explain that he couldn't right then, but that he would be glad to oblige when practice was through. And whenever possible, he took care of the fans. He never just said he would to put somebody off.

Time consuming as the fans' demands were, Aaron did not neglect his primary mission in Sun City. He reported to camp only a little overweight and worked out with the rest of us, taking no more liberties with his training schedule than would be expected of a man about to begin his twenty-second year of major league play. He worked on his swing until it sounded as though a machine, instead of a man, were rapping baseballs through the infield, into the outfield and often over the fence.

Even during the routine and tedious activities, such as wind sprints and exercises, Aaron held his head high. Sprinting across the outfield grass with a blue windbreaker under his team jersey and over a sweatshirt, his style and dedication were evident — nothing flashy, but, he worked hard to get ready to do what he does best. Aaron made just about all of the trips during the Cactus League exhibition season. He felt he had a responsibility to the team and to the fans in the other cities who wanted to see him play. And even though Manager Del Crandall said that he wasn't going to use his former teammate in any other role but that of designated hitter, Aaron spelled Johnny Briggs and Sixto Lezcano in the outfield on a number of occasions.

As I mentioned before, we began actual workouts on March 3, and for the first ten days or so, conditioning was the major concern. We had to be dressed and on the field each morning at 9:30, and the day would start with calisthenics for fifteen minutes. After that, we had about fifteen minutes' of running, followed by some football-type drills such as running backwards and sideways. Only then did we pick up our gloves. Early in camp we did "capers." These involved the infielders and outfielders — the pitchers worked by themselves on their own capers, pick-offs, covering first, etc. We did second-to-short and short-to-second flips, about twenty from each side. Later in the spring, we just threw the ball around to get our arms loose and ready. At about 11 each morning we took a break to change sweatshirts, and then it was back out for batting practice.

Batting practice usually lasted for about two hours, and since only one guy can hit at a time, it was fielding practice, too. By the time 30 or 40 guys had swung the bat, it was pretty close to two in the afternoon. Once the batting was done, we finished up with more running and then called it a day around 2:30.

The rest of the day was free. Whether it was recuperating from sore muscles, sightseeing, watching TV, playing cards, checking on things at home, taking clothes out to be cleaned, getting in a round of golf, or going out to dinner, our time was our own until midmorning the next day.

Even after spring training games began, the routine wasn't that much different. We still had to be at the park at 9:30, but when we got outside we did our own running and loosening up. That part of the program wasn't supervised by Del or the coaches any longer, so it was up to each player to stay in shape. Once that was finished, the coaching staff came out and had us work on different parts of the game. One day we'd work on rundowns, the next day we'd work with the outfielders on throwing to the cut-off man and relays. After those drills were completed, we'd hit for an hour or so, go back into the clubhouse to change sweatshirts, then return to the field and get ready for the game.

On days that we had a bus trip, the schedule varied just a little. We'd be at the park at the assigned time, dress, go outside and throw a little and then the guys going on the trip would take a few swings at the plate. By the time that brief workout was completed it would be nearly 11 o'clock, time to go back into the clubhouse, change sweatshirts, grab a quick bite to eat and then get on the bus and go.

Once in a while during a bus trip, you might look down at yourself and think back to your days of high school ball, when you dressed for the game at your school and climbed aboard one of those big yellow busses. The feeling in the spring can often be the same, but all you have to do is take a look at the front of your uniform shirt and see that it says, "Brewers," and not "LaPlata High."

The routine I have just described was the way the Brewers had us go through spring training in 1975 — Hank Aaron included. I'm sure Del told him to work at his own pace, but Henry did not take advantage of the situation. He might not have run as much as the rest of us, but he didn't run that much less, either. When it came time to shag balls for the other guys during batting practice, Aaron was in the outfield. When we ran the bases, so did Henry. There wasn't even a hint in Arizona that he wasn't putting out a 100 percent effort. Each time he had the uniform on, I think he set an example for the entire club to follow.

Another thing that impressed me about our most celebrated player was the rather low profile he presented while on the field, and even in the community. He did not try for any role that would suddenly thrust him into a position of leadership. In fact, I really don't think we came away from Arizona with what you would call a team leader. We did elect Mike Hegan our representative to the Major League Players' Association, but that was something we had to do, since our player rep from 1974 — Johnny Vukovich — had been traded to the Cincinnati Reds.

As I've said, Aaron did give us an example to follow by the way he went through camp, just like a guy hustling to make the club. And he did conduct a hitting clinic for all of us.

Aaron's presentation of the clinic was at the request of Del Crandall. Henry was assisted by our batting coach, Harvey Kuenn. Although Harvey was a pretty fair country hitter in his day — big plug of chewing tobacco and all — I don't think he minded when this particular student took over the teaching role. In fact, Del told us he was going to use Henry like this sometimes during the regular season, and I was surprised to learn that Aaron had never even been asked by the management of the Braves to help with hitting. If Hank Aaron doesn't know about hitting, then nobody does. And any coach or manager who can't use the experience of such a player is wasting a lot of talent.

The hitting clinic (we all attended) lasted about an hour and dealt mainly with little tips on batting. Henry's main message was about plate performance, but I think what he said also had a lot to do with his own philosophy about the entire game of baseball. He explained to us that he had had to learn to hit differently from time to time in his years in the big leagues, and that it was his willingness to make adjustments in his swing and style of play that enabled him to stay around so long. When he first came up to the big leagues, he said, he held his hands high. But then as he got older, he had to drop them and bring them in closer to his body so that his swinging motion would not be wasted. But there was more to his talk than just how and where to hold the bat.

Henry also talked about discipline — thinking about the game of baseball whenever you are out on the field in all kinds of situations. It may be, he said, that when you are at bat, moving the runners over with a bunt or a single will be just as good as or better than swinging for the fences. Or another time, you may be looking for a 2 and 0 fastball and instead the pitcher throws you a curve right down the middle. The disciplined ballplayer would not swing at the curve because he wasn't looking for it, no matter how good it looked coming over the plate, Hank said. He also talked about knowing what to expect from certain pitchers in certain situations, what kinds of things a guy can do to protect the plate when a man on first has the ability to steal, and how a guy can help his club at bat even if he isn't a great hitter.

All of these things are rules and fundamentals we had been taught at one time or another in our careers, but hearing them from Aaron made a difference. Now I'm not saying that if Harvey Kuenn had told us the same things, we'd have passed them off.

But a guy like Aaron is the proof of the rule and the example to follow. He does things the way they are supposed to be done, and as a result he knows how they should be taught. Even if that seminar helped only one guy to better understand, not only his hitting but himself as a ballplayer, it was well worth the time and effort.

One of the good points Aaron brought up in his talk was that even though you get older, you still can play the game. What this had to do with the immediate futures of the younger guys was not that important, but it may mean something to them later, when they have become veteran ballplayers. It will give them something to think back on when the time comes for them to make the same kinds of adjustments and decisions that Hank has had to make. I don't consider myself, at 28, old by any means, but I have had to change my stroke once already in my career, and probably will have to again. But as Henry said, as you get older, you've got to go with the pitches. He has done pretty well in that respect and in more ways than hitting home runs, too.

Speaking of home runs, Henry hit only one in Cactus League play. It was almost at the end of our spring training schedule, off the San Diego Padres' Sonny Siebert on April 2, during a game that we won by 5-1.

I remember I had the feeling that some fans were surprised that Aaron got his first game situation homer so late in spring training. That did not reflect the feelings of either the club or Henry. Spring training is a time for getting into the groove for the coming season. Most of the time, guys don't want to reach a real peak until just about the time camp is ready to break. The idea in the spring is not to press, but to just make the good kind of contact that you want to make all season long. Power hitters like Aaron aren't interested in pounding the ball out in March. They're more interested in being ready to do the job once the season starts.

I will say, though, that most of the players and fans felt pretty good about seeing Henry hit his first one out.

I learned an interesting sidelight to Aaron and his hitting during the spring. When he first came up to the big leagues, he had a difficult time trying to find a bat that was right for him. Most of us, at one time or another, have had the same thing happen to us. And most of us did just what Aaron did. He scrounged around in the dugout, among his teammates' bats, until he found one that felt right. And as things turned out, Henry did have a fair amount of success with that bat of one of his old Milwaukee Braves teammates. With the exception of some slight changes made over the years, Hank Aaron is still using the same model bat — a bat that was lent to him many years ago by a catcher named Del Crandall. And when Aaron broke Babe Ruth's career home run mark, he had on a pair of spikes that he had somehow acquired from Joe Pepitone. So you could say that Hank's skill at the plate is the result of his ability — and maybe just a little help from his friends.

About the only thing Hank really did any different from the rest of us was to stay at the Kings Inn Hotel — the place where the management also stayed. But he did that only because of a club rule that required all players who had brought their wives to camp to stay at another location, away from the rest of the team.

Having his wife in camp kind of kept Hank away from the rest of us during most of the off-hours. He wanted to be with her just as much as we'd have liked to have been with our wives if they had been with us. But there were occasions when he, too, was involved in some after-practice activity. Besides the half-dozen times we all went out to play golf, there were bull sessions in the clubhouse, and those general get-togethers ballplayers are fond of. Henry Aaron enjoyed them, too, for no matter how much you love the game or have been a part of it, it's nice to get away from what takes place between the foul lines once in a while, even if it's just sitting in the locker room, chewing the fat.

I'd have to rate our 1975 spring training camp as a good one. Del and the coaches ran the club just as they would have without the addition of a big name star, so there was not a lot of friction. Also on the plus side, the club dropped its policy against mustaches.

About 80 percent of us left Arizona with something growing on our upper lips, and although the new growth looked better on some than on others, the real value in the lifting of the ban was a more relaxed attitude. In the past, certain players had complained about not being able to sport facial hair, especially when other teams were sprouting the stuff in what seemed to be hedges.

Mustaches aside, I think we looked good in Arizona — even better than we had in 1974. Because of some injuries, Del wasn't able to play his starting lineup until the last exhibition game, but we had a .500 record for the 24 games we played in the Cactus League. I felt we were in pretty good shape for the start of the season. Our pitching, which had been our only real question mark at the beginning of March, looked real good. Pete Broberg — a guy we had picked up from the Texas Rangers over the winter — had a pretty decent spring. Jim Slaton and Billy Champion also did well when they got in, and Ed Sprague and Jim Colborn seemed to have come off their knee operations in good shape and appeared to be buys we could count on.

We averaged about 2,500-3,000 fans at our games, mostly because Henry Aaron was in the line-up. But we fielded a representative and competitive team, and I think that had something to do with it, too. Once we even played before an overflow crowd of better than 6,000 in Tucson when we faced the Cleveland Indians. The appearances of Aaron and

Frank Robinson on the same field helped pull the people in — and a couple of thousand more were turned away.

Aaron was going to be a big factor in our drawing power, and, even though we left Sun City without any lefthanded pitching, I felt that the team was capable of playing better than .500 baseball. Based on the competition in the East Division of the American League over the past couple of years, I felt that any season mark in that area would put us well up in the standings. We were looking forward to a big season.

Chapter 4

Welcome Home Henry

We opened our season on April 8, in Boston's
Fenway Park. The weather in Massachusetts was
cold and damp. In fact, there was still some snow on
the ground in parts of town, a reminder of a storm
that had moved up the Eastern Seaboard just a couple of days before our arrival. But the day of Boston's
home opener was clear, and a crowd of over 34,000
fans filled the stands to see the Brewers and the Red
Sox meet in the first game of the new baseball year.

For the Boston fans, there seemed to be two chief
points of interest. The first was Hank Aaron, making
his American League debut in their town, and the
second was Tony Conigliaro, returning to baseball in
a Red Sox uniform. Tony C. had been out of baseball
for 3½ years because of problems stemming from an

eye injury in 1967, an injury that was thought to have ended his playing career. Both Hank and Tony were in the lineups as designated hitters, and both got fine ovations during pre-game ceremonies. In fact, it was hard to tell just who was the real hometown favorite.

Aaron's first appearance at bat in the American League was greeted with a round of applause, but Luis Tiant did not allow that reaction to change his pitching style. He kept the ball away from Henry and our DH reached base for the first time in his new league career on a walk. The next three times up, Aaron struck out once and grounded out twice. His stats at the end of the day went down in the books as 0 for 3.

Conigliaro had a slightly better day. In four times at bat, he hit a single. That put him on base and enabled him to work a double steal with Carl Yastrzemski and give the Sox a run in the first inning. The final score was Boston, 5-2. Our only extra base hits came from George Scott, Johnny Briggs and myself with doubles, and from Robin Yount, who hit a home run.

Afterward, our locker room was filled with reporters who wanted to get the inside story on how Mr. H. Aaron felt after playing his first game in the American League. Henry didn't wait for the questions, he volunteered his own answers to just about anything the writers might possibly have wanted to know.

No, he said, the big wall in left field hadn't bothered him at all. And, no, he didn't think that it was too cold out on the field. In fact, Aaron told the writers that he thought it was rather nice. He also said that he didn't mind being the club's designated hitter, and that not playing in the field didn't really bother him.

One of the writers asked him about the way Tiant had been pitching to him all day — mostly low and away. Henry said that the low balls didn't bother him too much. "I'm a lowball hitter and a highball drinker," he said with a chuckle.

The next day we played another afternoon game against the Red Sox, only this time the crowd dropped down to around 7,000. Scotty and Yount were our hitting leaders as they drove in two runs each in our 7-4 victory. Pete Broberg got credit for his first win of the year and Tom Murphy picked up his first save. Henry got some more junk to swing at and had another 0 for 3 day. That night we got on the plane and headed back for our home opener in Milwaukee.

There are at least two big days in the life of a ballplayer every season. One is Opening Day on the road. The other, even bigger, is Opening Day at home. No matter how many seasons a player has experienced, each start of a new campaign lingers in the memory.

To a rookie, the start of a new season may be the beginning of a great career. It also may be the start of one that lasts for no more than a very short time. For the veteran, each new season is another chapter in his history as a big league ball player.

Some opening day performances will be better than others, but each one amounts to the first paragraph of a seasonal story that is hoped will be the best one written in the history of the game.

Thoughts often spin through your head as you sit in the locker room during the first few days of the year. Which guys will still be with the club after 162 games? What about the personality change of the club as its fortunes go up or down? Just how much will you, personally, add to whatever successes the club will experience before the division races are through?

The start of a new season is filled with anticipation. And that was especially true for us as we prepared for our home opener against the Cleveland Indians on Friday, April 11.

This was kind of a different home opener for me and, I would hazard to say, for the rest of the guys on the club and the fans in the Milwaukee area, too. Almost from that day in November of 1974 that Hank Aaron signed with our club, the attentions of our fans had been focused on this date.

Almost before the ink was dry on Aaron's contract, Dick Hackett, our ticket director, was swamped with requests for season ticket and Opening Day ticket information. Dick even commented once in January that fans were writing letters to thank the club for bringing Henry back to Milwaukee and enclosing them along with their ticket information requests. The interest in Opening Day was well above what could be considered normal, even for the most rabid baseball fans.

The big weekend actually got started for us the day before we were to take the field for the first time at home. The team attended a welcome-back-to-town luncheon. Aaron complimented the people of the area for their long-time support of him as a player, and he even said they had been responsible for much of his success. He and his remarks were received warmly, and he set the stage for one of the greatest opening days in the recent history of the game.

Going to the stadium for the first home game of the season has always been something kind of special to me. The feeling of what is about to happen during the next few hours makes the day seem a real occasion.

As usual, we had to be at the ball park well before game time. But it always seems that no matter how early you arrive, there are always people milling around the stadium waiting for the gates to open or trying to get an extra ticket or two. And on the first day of our '75 season, the early arrival of the crowd ran true to form.

Driving in from the expressway to the player parking lot, I got a good long view of the early fans and the stadium, a massive steel, aluminum, brick and concrete structure. Only the flapping of the colorful flags and banners drew my attention away from the size of the building that for 81 games each season is called home. I made my way into the clubhouse amidst the noise of vendors preparing for what would probably be one of their biggest selling days of the year.

The locker room was beginning to fill up with players and coaches, and the sight of the home whites hanging in each cubicle was a sure sign that this was the day everyone had been waiting for. Dressing took no longer than it ever had before, but pulling on the white doubleknits of the host team made all the difference in the world as to the meaning of the day.

Stepping out onto the County Stadium playing field for the first time of the new season, I heard the sounds of fans calling for autographs and vendors going through the park shouting, "Program! . . . Get your Opening Day program, here! . . . Take home a souvenir of the return of Henry Aaron! . . . Program! . . ." The sounds seemed to echo in every corner of the stands, and the exchange of money for the scorecard looked like something even a fast dealing card player would have had trouble keeping up with.

We took our infield and batting practice, the Indians did the same and then both teams went to the dugout before the start of the pre-game ceremonies. The weather was typical Wisconsin for early April — clear and cold with the temperature at game time an unbaseball-like 37 degrees. The fans, though, came in record numbers, despite the cold. In all, 48,160 of them were in the stands to welcome us back to town, a total that broke our attendance record of 46,812, which had been set the previous June when we played the Oakland A's. In fact, the total was just 482 short of bettering the all-time league game attendance for County Stadium, which was set when the Braves and Phillies played back in September of 1959. In their stocking caps and with their heavy blankets wrapped around them, though, the fans looked more like a crowd in December, out to see the Green Bay Packers play.

The introduction of Commissioner Bowie Kuhn, American League President Lee MacPhail and Milwaukee County Executive John Doyne stirred the first Bronx Cheers of the year. Then the Cleveland Indians were introduced, with manager Frank Robinson, the first black manager in the majors, receiving a nice ovation. Frank, also the Indians' designated hitter, had hit a home run in his first time up at Cleveland's home opener. When it was our turn to take the field, the stadium just about exploded.

Earl Gillespie, the former radio voice of the Milwaukee Braves, introduced each of us, and every player was given the kind of welcome you would expect a hometown performer to get. The last man on Earl's list was Aaron, and when he stepped out, the fans gave him an ovation that must have lasted for two or three minutes. And then, to add to the greeting, the fans sang to Henry to the tune of "Hello,

Dolly." Most of us sang along:

> *"Welcome home, Henry,*
> *Welcome home, Henry.*
> *It's so nice to have you back*
> *Where you belong."*

The welcome was just fantastic, and the fans' feelings for Aaron were obvious. Through a sea of newspaper and television cameramen, Henry stepped to a microphone at home plate and thanked the throng for the tremendous welcome. He told them again of the special place Milwaukee had in his heart and said he hoped he could help write a new chapter in the history of Milwaukee baseball. Again, the fans gave him a standing ovation as he headed back to our dugout and we prepared to play the first inning of the new baseball season at home.

The scoring started for us in the third inning, when Johnny Briggs hit a single to right that moved Bob Coluccio over to third. Coluccio had reached base on a walk by Jim Perry, and he scored our first run when Aaron hit a fielder's choice grounder to Ed Crosby at shortstop.

Cleveland tied the game in the fourth when Charlie Spikes singled, Boog Powell just walked and Buddy Bell sent a hit past me at third.

Then, in the bottom of the sixth inning, we scored five runs. Briggs started it when he hit Perry's 2-2 pitch over the right field wall. Then Aaron came up, hit a long foul into the left field seats, took a ball, fouled off two more pitches and finally hit one into the hole at short for a single.

It wasn't a homer, but it was Hank's first hit as a Brewer after eight previous appearances at the plate, and the crowd was duly appreciative.

With two outs, Frank Robinson ordered Perry to walk Darrell Porter, so that Perry could work on Sixto Lezcano. But our rookie right fielder came through with a single up the middle that scored Aaron and prompted the removal of Jim Perry in favor of relief pitcher Dick Bosman.

Pedro Garcia was up next, and with him in the box we went through what one of the papers in town called a "nondouble steal." Lezcano broke for second and Johnny Ellis, the Indians' catcher, threw the ball to Jack Brohamer, who was covering the play. Lezcano was trapped between second and first, and while Sixto was wondering which way to go, Darrell Porter thought he'd take a couple of steps off third base. Brohamer saw Porter off the bag and tried to nail him. But Brohamer's throw to Bell was high and wide. Porter got back to third, and Lezcano finally made it to second. All hands remained safe.

Garcia then hit Bosman's next pitch for a double down the left field line, scoring both Porter and Lezcano. Robin Yount hit a shot to short and reached first when Crosby's throw drew Powell off the bag. And while the Indians were chasing the errant throw, Garcia scored our final run of the day from second.

The Indians came back to score one more run in

the ninth. Ellis hit a single to right, then with two out, Brohamer hit a shot into the hole in short right. Garcia made a great play to get the ball but threw it a bit short to Scott at first and Brohamer was on. Crosby then doubled to right to score Ellis and move Brohamer over to third. Del put Tom Murphy in to relieve our starter, Billy Champion, and Tom pitched to the last batter, getting the side out. The first win of the season at home was ours.

So that was the game. The 6-2 victory was pleasing to the fans. Billy Champion pitched 8 2/3 innings of good ball and earned his first win of the year. And our first home victory of the season moved us into first place in the American League's Eastern Division, so the fans went away looking ahead to an exciting season of baseball.

As for Henry Aaron, he had walked, gotten his first American League hit, scored his first American League run, and recorded his first American League run batted in, an RBI that totaled number 2,203 in his career and put him just six short of the record held by Babe Ruth.

Outside in the stadium, the day had been Aaron's. But in the locker room, he tried to put the game into proper perspective.

"Why don't you guys go talk to John Briggs?" Henry asked the crowd of newsmen surrounding his locker. "And go talk to Billy Champion. He pitched a fine game. We've got a fine young team here. I just want to be part of it."

I think Hank was a little embarrassed by all of the attention. And maybe even just a little sorry that after getting his first hit, he had tried to steal second base. The steal was unsuccessful, but it was the kind of surprising thing that put a hint of a smile on everyone's face, since it proved that Henry Aaron was still interested in playing the game. No matter how we had done on the field or how Aaron had performed that day, April 11, 1975, in Milwaukee County Stadium belonged to Henry Aaron.

The next day we played another afternoon game with the Indians before a crowd of about 11,500. We won that game, 6-5, with quite a bit of help in the hitting department from some of the younger guys.

Sixto Lezcano drove in two runs with a homer and a double, and Robin Yount hit his second homer of the year. We got to Fritz Peterson early in the game as we scored four runs in the first, and one each in the second and the third. The Indians got homers from Boog Powell, who hit two, and George Hendrick. Jim Slaton got the win with help from Ed Sprague and Tom Murphy. Aaron went 1 for 3, hitting a double.

The last game of the series, on Sunday, went to the Indians as Gaylord Perry, Jim's brother, recorded his 200th major league victory, 3-1. Gaylord Perry's victory at our expense made him only the 70th man in the history of baseball to record that many victories.

The series, though, was a good one for us. We won two of the three games, something that is always nice. But I think it was a series everyone was glad to see over. Now that Hank Aaron had returned home to Milwaukee, the pressure was off.

I'll bet most of the fans who saw us play that weekend had little on their minds whenever Aaron came up other than that he was the home run champ of all time, and that maybe he would put one out of the park.

It's almost impossible not to think of home runs when you think of Henry Aaron and the time it took him to catch and pass Babe Ruth's total of 714 homers. I had always been interested in what Hank's feelings might have been about breaking that record, but I had never felt comfortable about just going up to him and asking. Then one day, not long after our season opener, Henry and I were just sitting in the clubhouse, talking about baseball, and he brought it up.

I asked him if he had ever thought, when he started twenty-one years ago, that he would end up doing as well as he has. Henry thought for just a moment. He said that when he came up to the big leagues, he had no goals in mind. All he wanted to do then was go out each day and play the best he could. He really had not given the home run record much real thought he said, until 1969, when he hit 44 homers for a total of 554. It was then, he said, that he felt he might be able to pass Ruth.

One of the things he said had helped him in hitting all those home runs was his good health. He never was injured to any great extent, and so he never missed much playing time. He said that playing in good hitting parks, such as County Stadium when he first played there, or in Atlanta Stadium after the Braves had moved to Georgia, were other plus factors. And, Hank said he had been fortunate to play most of his career with good hitting clubs. That gave him a better chance to hit the long ball. When a club has a lot of heavy hitters in the lineup, it's hard for another team to pitch around one guy to get an easier out, since there aren't many easy outs. But when a team has a weak hitting lineup, it's fairly easy for the competition to pitch around a strong hitter. You don't have to worry too much about the next guy coming to bat and taking you over the wall. The guys batting around you in the lineup have a lot to do with your own performance at the plate.

I asked Henry if he thought there was any chance his home run mark would ever be broken. To my surprise, he said he thought that a couple of guys "on the Philadelphia club" had a chance. Aaron didn't mention any names, but the only guys with the Phillies who have the ability to hit home runs in that number are Greg Luzinski and Mike Schmidt. In my opinion, though, whatever Aaron's total is when he finally does leave the game, it should survive for an awfully long time.

That chance conversation I had with Henry was probably one of the few times he has talked with anyone on the club about his career. Whenever he did mention something about his past, though, he always had a very matter-of-fact attitude and left the impression that he had been fortunate that the honors, records and achievements could have happened to a pretty fair country baseball player from Mobile, Alabama.

Chapter 5

On the Road Again

With the Milwaukee portion of the season success-
fully underway, we hit the road again, on a seven day
trip that took us to Baltimore, for a two-game series
with the Orioles, and Cleveland, where we were
scheduled to play three games over the weekend.

We got into Baltimore a day early and the weather
wasn't bad. But on game day, the skies turned dark
and gloomy. It rained for most of the morning, then
tailed off into an intermittent drizzle in the afternoon.
Our game was at night, so most of us kept an eye on
the sky and an ear on the radio.

There were no reports of a postponement, though,
and late in the afternoon we boarded our bus at the

motel and headed for the park. At best, it was going to be cold and damp, and the attendance would be down. But some hardy fans in town wanted to see the game, and as we got off the bus at the ballpark, some were arriving to join those waiting for the gates to open.

The rain had stopped but we learned that there probably wouldn't be any infield or batting practice. The ground crew wanted to keep the tarpaulin on the field for as long as possible. We slipped into our powder blue doubleknits, had a short team meeting and headed for the dugout and our first look at the Baltimore field for the year.

I talked to a reporter for a few minutes, then made my way through the dugout and stepped onto the field to join a group of guys playing pepper to loosen up. A ball from another bunch of players went down the first base line near me, and as I stepped away from my group to retrieve it, I noticed a crowd of about fifteen or twenty fans pushing to get closer to the rail in short right field. Henry Aaron was there, standing on a soggy warning track, reaching over a rolled up tarp to sign autographs.

Hank had on one of our lined nylon warmup jackets and I could see his blue-clad figure moving back and forth in an area of about two feet as he reached for the items the fans wanted signed — programs, gloves, balls and photographs. Some of the pictures were mounted on colored paper and looked as if they had been cut out of "Sports Illustrated". The fans seemed an orderly group, waiting their turns to meet the man who had become the most sought after player in the game today. Kids with stocking caps and Instamatic cameras squeezed to the front of the group and flashcubes popped at a rate that made me wish I owned a large block of Kodak stock.

Henry tried to get to everyone, but the crowd kept growing, and when he felt he had done as much as he could to satisfy the throng, he excused himself and headed back to our dugout. He was deluged with calls and pleas from the stands of, "Sign just one more, Henry! Just one more!!" But Aaron, like the rest of us, had to get ready for the game.

After warmups I headed back to the clubhouse to change into my game shoes and to get my game glove. But just before I reached the dugout, I noticed some friends in the stands and went over to say hello. While I was at the rail, some fans came over and asked for my autograph and then said in almost the same breath, ". . . and can you get Hank Aaron to sign it, too?"

I think just about all of the guys went through that experience. Even a couple of the writers on the field before the game had fans wanting them to go into the clubhouse and get Henry to sign a ball, a pennant or the day's program. One fellow had a list of names on a pad that a fan wanted Aaron to sign. The interest in our designated hitter was amazing. The crowd on this dreary night was announced at just 6,706, but I think

I must have seen or talked to just about all of the fans in their efforts to get a bit closer to the player who a year before had made baseball history!

There were a lot of sports writers in the park, just as there were for each of our first games in the rest of the cities in the league. Writers from as far away as Pennsylvania and New Jersey were at our game in Baltimore, and a large contingent of television and newspaper photographers was also on hand. Cameramen are allowed on the playing field while the game is in progress. They are no bother to the players or play on the field. But I was interested to discover that a couple of guys from the Baltimore Bicentennial Committee were on hand to specially record this game — the first appearance there for Henry Aaron — American Leaguer.

As the visiting team, we were up first, and when Aaron moved out to the on-deck circle, we could hear a slight ripple of applause build from the seats directly behind us. Then, as Henry stepped to the plate to face Jim Palmer, the public address announcer began, "For the Milwaukee Brewers . . . the designated hitter . . . number 44 . . . Henry Aaron . . . ." But before the introduction was over, the fans were on their feet, giving Hank the kind of welcome usually reserved for one of their own team's stars.

Hank didn't get much to swing at all night, though, and went 0 for 3. He did get an intentional walk in the eighth inning, but then was taken out for pinch runner Bobby Mitchell. That walk loaded the bases, though, and was just one of the nice things that happened in that inning. We scored six runs and beat the Orioles, 7-1.

Winning made up for the bad weather. The temperature at game time was announced as 45 degrees, but nobody said whether that was above or below zero. On nights like these, guys do all kinds of things to keep warm. Some suit up over a set of long johns. I never do, but I always wear a long sleeved baseball undershirt, whatever the weather.

I can remember sitting on the bench while we were at bat with a jacket over my legs. To my left was a bundled up Timmy Johnson, and on my right sat catcher Darrell Porter with a hot water bottle in his hands, trying to keep them warm. Sometimes guys not playing drink hot soup or coffee to try to keep the chill off, but most of the time those not playing take refuge in the tunnel or runway leading back into the clubhouse. That's especially true on the cold, damp nights when water covers the floor of the dugout, and the walls are slick with moisture.

I also noticed something about Aaron's manner during the early games that changed once the weather got warmer. When it was cold, Henry kept his batting helmet on all the time in the on-deck circle, and went directly into the batter's box without much more by way of loosening up than just throwing the leaded bat back to the bat boy. Then he set himself and was ready for the first pitch.

When it got warmer, Aaron carried his bat and his

helmet out to the on-deck circle, picked up the weighted bat, took a couple of swings with the two pieces of lumber and then knelt down on his right knee to wait his turn to hit. When he moved up to the plate, Henry picked up his helmet, took his bats to the home plate area, squashed the plastic helmet on over his cap, stepped into the box, planted his feet, and took a practice swing or two. When the weather is warm, there is no big hurry.

But trying to stay comfortable is difficult in the early season, especially if you aren't playing and have to spend time riding the bench. Guys in the bullpen are in the same situation, but at least they have a little notice before they go into the game and have a chance to warm up. Designated hitters, like Aaron, have it a little tougher. They are semi-active during the game, but in cold weather that's not enough to keep them warm or as ready to hit as a guy on the field.

I think that Henry was even a bit concerned about that before the start of the season. He wanted to find out what the rest of the designated hitters did between times at bat. I've seen some guys swing a bat during the whole time their team was in the field. Others would go back into the tunnel or clubhouse to do exercises. Orlando Cepeda, during the first year of the DH rule in the American League, had an exercise bike handy to ride between innings. Just about every DH has his own method of being ready. Henry tried to stay loose and keep mentally in the game.

I think the mental attitude of the DH has to be something a little different from, and a shade more important than that of the rest of the players on the team. Not playing makes it hard to keep your mind right with the action and there is a tendency to get stale between times at bat.

But although the DH does have it a little tougher than, say, a relief pitcher, who either does the job or is taken out, the guy with the toughest job of all in baseball is the pinch hitter. Terry Harmon, a utility player with the Phillies, once gave me a great definition of a pinch hitter. He said, "A utility player on a ball club is just like the spare tire in the trunk of your car. You are hoping you don't have to use him, but when you do, you want him to do the job." I think that definition more than fits the pinch hitter, the guy you send into the game to do just one thing, get a needed hit in the pinch.

Well, anyway, we did beat the Orioles on that cold night, but they came back the next night and shut us out, 2-0. We left Baltimore the next day for our first weekend road series and our second meeting in a week against Frank Robinson's Cleveland Indians.

We opened with a Friday afternoon game and it turned out to be the game Henry was looking for. He hit his first American League home run, and he started to look better at the plate. He went 2 for 3, breaking a hitless streak that had gone on for a dozen at bats.

We were ahead, 1-0, when Johnny Briggs set the

stage for Hank's homer by sending one out of the park himself in the sixth inning. Aaron was the next batter, and he too sent Gaylord Perry over the wall on a 1-2 pitch to give us a 3-zip margin.

The Indians came back with a run on George Hendrick's homer in the bottom of the inning, but Henry drove in another for us by singling home Robin Yount in the eighth. We scored another run in the ninth and beat the Indians, 5-1.

After hitting his first American League home run and Number 734 of his career, Aaron reacted as always. He rounded the bases, came into the dugout and received a standard major league welcome. I think he was more pleased going 2 for 3 than he was in getting that long hit, because he had been struggling.

In fact, Hank's slow start had become a pretty warm topic for the press corps. He seemed a little disturbed that some writers had suggested putting him out to pasture. One Baltimore writer wrote that Aaron was all through as a player and ought to just retire. Fan and journalistic reaction like that to a man who has devoted as much of his life to something as Hank Aaron has strikes me as nothing more than jealousy. Aaron, though, said that despite his achievements, some people still weren't satisfied and he had to keep on proving himself in their eyes. I guess he felt like a gunfighter in the Old West. Whenever he went into a new town there was always some young hand who was ready to challenge the man and take away the title of top gun. Being the greatest home run hitter in baseball, you always are open to challenges, which are good since they keep interest in the game and develop new heroes for new generations of fans.

I have to give Aaron a lot of credit for the way he handled himself with the press. Wherever we went, Hank had to face the same questions, phrased the same way and reported almost exactly as they had been reported in another town just a day or two before. Mostly, the writers and broadcasters were interested in Aaron's career before he came with us, and they were all certainly interested in the home runs he had put into the record book. It must have been tiring for him to hear the same questions and give the same answers hundreds and hundreds of times. He really held up well, and often answered questions at times that he probably just wanted to be left alone.

We beat Cleveland again on Saturday, then lost on Sunday. Aaron didn't get any hits in either game, although he did have an RBI in our 7-4 loss Sunday. Still, we had taken 2 out of 3 from the Indians again and we left Ohio for Milwaukee in second place.

We were scheduled to play the Orioles the next night on NBC-TV's "Monday Night Baseball" program, but a weather front moved in and brought with it another rain to float us right out of the view of a national television audience. When we finally did get to play the first game of the two game set the next night, Jim Palmer allowed only six hits and the

Orioles beat us, 1-0. Aaron continued to have problems at the plate, and before gametime the next night, asked Del to replace him in the lineup.

I don't think anyone was more surprised to be in the lineup on April 24, than Bobby Mitchell. He had performed for us as a DH in other years, but his subbing for Aaron must have been the last thing on his mind as he got ready to come to the park that night. Surprised or not, Bobby went out and hit two doubles and scored two runs as we came from behind to beat the Orioles, 8-5.

Afterward, the inevitable horde of reporters came into the clubhouse asking why Aaron had not been in the lineup. Henry said that he wanted someone else to play because he didn't think that his .114 batting average was doing much to help the club. He told the reporters quite simply, "I'm not hitting." Del told how Aaron had asked to be rested for a couple of days and gave Mitchell a pat on the back for coming into the game and doing the job after not having batted once in our first eleven games.

Aaron's taking himself out of the lineup was something that impressed a lot of us on the ball club. He was having a rather bad time at the plate, and when that situation comes up, it often is a good idea to just sit in the dugout for a couple of days, relax, watch the pitchers more comfortably and get back your perspective.

I think one of the reasons Hank was struggling was that he hadn't hit a home run in our own ball park. In fact, it took him until June 12, during a game against the Oakland A's, before he straightened out one of those long left field fouls and finally made "Bernie Brewer" — our club mascot who sits in a chalet high up in the center field stands — slide down from his perch into the huge beer stein. That's the start of our home run display. Henry's first blast out of County Stadium since 1965 was number 739 in his career and his 185th official shot out of the park. By making the home fans happy, he took some pressure off himself and began to go to the plate without subconsciously pressing. Pressing is one of the curses a guy carries with him when he is famous for doing one thing and he wants to please the fans by doing it. The shame of it is that Aaron could have gone the entire year without hitting a homer in County Stadium, could have hit a zillion singles and doubles to help us win games, and there still would have been a few fans who would not have been satisfied until he hit a home run for them.

89

Henry's taking himself out of the lineup automatically put him in a special class. Lots of players won't do it. They just keep struggling, continue to hurt themselves, and do little of value for the club. Aaron did the hard thing, not only because of the kind of man he is, but also because he wants to win. He's part of the club and it takes the efforts of all twenty-five of us to win. Eight or nine guys can't do it alone. These efforts could be making a game saving catch, turning in a good performance in a pinch situation or just putting aside personal feelings or ego for the good of the club. No matter what they are, they should be aimed at the betterment of the team. Aaron showed me a lot when he took himself out of the lineup, hoping that by doing so he could help the team.

After our short homestand with the Orioles, we packed our bags again and traveled to New York City for the beginning of a weekend four game series with the Yankees. Rain plagued us again and our Friday night game was postponed. But Saturday was a crisp spring day and enabled us to get our first look at the Yanks. And, boy, did we get a good look at them. They swatted our pitching all over the place in a thirteen hit attack and won, 10-1. It was one of those games we were glad to see end.

But even though we lost, Hank Aaron was responsible for a big thrill for the fans in Shea Stadium that afternoon. The rest that Aaron had asked for a couple of days earlier must have done him some good. He hit one of Pat Dobson's seventh inning pitches 442 feet over the left center field wall to give us our only run. It was his first regular season home run against Babe Ruth's old club, although he had hit three against the Yankees in the 1957 World Series with the Braves. Henry also had a single that day to make his 2 for 4 outing at the plate the best effort for our team.

On Sunday, we played a doubleheader before a Cap Day crowd of well over 41,000. In the first game, which we won, 7-0, Henry tied Babe Ruth's RBI record of 2,209 for a career when he drove in two runs with a bases loaded double in the seventh. He got another standing ovation when the announcement was made over the loudspeaker and flashed on the scoreboard. His accomplishment meant something to every ballplayer on the field that day, too. We all know how hard it is sometimes just to move a guy from first to second.

Editor's Note: Ruth's record at the time was incorrectly listed. In February of 1976, baseball's Official Records Committee announced the discovery of clerical errors. The adjustment dropped Ruth's total from 2,209 to 2,204, still good for a second place on the all-time list. Aaron had 2,262 RBI going into the 1976 season.

After the second game, which we lost, 10-1, Henry was beseiged again by reporters. They wanted to know how he felt about going up to bat with a chance to tie one of the Babe's marks while playing against Ruth's old team. Aaron said, as he calmly ate a cup of ice cream, that all he wanted to do was get a hit and try to help the club win another ball game. There wasn't any more to it than that.

He's right, too. That's the main thing — winning the ball game. The records are certainly nice to have, but you don't press to get them, especially when to do so would sacrifice a chance for your team to win. If it's late in the season, with only a few games left to go and some mark is in sight, a guy may go out and play with the idea that he needs only so many more of something or another to get into the books. But early in the season, you have to be more concerned with staying at the top or not letting those teams in the first division get too much of a lead on you. And if you play long enough and well enough, the records can be yours.

After the Yankee series, it was back to Milwaukee again for a series with the Detroit Tigers. On the last day of April, we stopped the Tigers' five game winning streak, 6-2. Then, on the first day of May, we really shellacked Detroit, 17-3, and moved into first place in our division!

I was starting to hit a little better myself, and when I was taken out of the game in the late innings, so that Kurt Bevacqua could get some playing time, I had enjoyed a 3 for 5 afternoon, scored two runs and had an RBI. But no one on our club had a day like that of our designated hitter. Once more, his name went into the major league record books.

Henry had a perfect day, 4 for 4! And in the process, he not only scored once himself, he also singled across Sixto Lezcano in the third inning to raise his RBI total one above Ruth's previous career record of 2,209. Then he added to his own mark in the fifth with an RBI double.

More reporters, more accolades for Aaron after the game, but all he could do was point to our kid shortstop and tell of the great day Yount had also had. At the time, Robin was one of the leading hitters in the league with a .387 average and he had finished the afternoon with four RBI's on a homer and a double.

Henry told the reporters that there were no more records within his reach, but that he felt good that he was even able to be considered in the company of such a great slugger as Babe Ruth. Henry said that he was glad that the pressure of erasing all of Ruth's batting records was finally over. Now it would be a little easier to just play baseball. The ball Hank hit for his 2,210 RBI was sent to the Hall of Fame in Cooperstown, New York, and the RBI's kept coming.

Chapter 6

Staying Loose

As I have tried to point out, on our first trips into each of the American League cities, Hank was the main attraction. People wanted to see him, and they wanted to see him hit home runs. In some cities the fans were more receptive than in others, and in some places the demands on Aaron's time weren't as severe as in others. But the one thing I'll say about our first swing through the league cities was that we at least had the opportunity to play baseball under major league conditions. Such was not the case, however, when we faced the Atlanta Braves in an exhibition game on May 5, in Memphis.

We had just finished a weekend series with the Yankees and were due to start on a two week trip after the exhibition game. It was billed as a game matching Henry Aaron against his former Atlanta teammates, but it was a flop from several standpoints. Only 11,365 fans showed up. Now that's not a bad crowd, but from the way the promoters were talking up the game, I kind of expected to see the stadium filled.

The game was played in Memorial Stadium, a football field and the home of the Liberty Bowl game. Just for this game, the field was converted into a baseball diamond. Turf was cut out of the field for the bases and pitcher's mound, and we had a right field fence — or as we called it, deep second — only 173 feet away from home plate. The left field wall, however, looked good for about a $2.50 taxi ride.

We really didn't want to play this game. We figured that someone could get hurt playing on a poorly prepared field, and for nothing. We had a meeting in the clubhouse before the game and decided that, although we did have to play, we didn't have to take any unnecessary chances. And so everyone would remember, we set up a fine system. Trying to steal a base would cost a player a dollar. So would sliding, or taking a strike at the plate. Our idea was to play the game, but to get it over fast, and without any stupid injuries.

The conditions were really bad. The field was in sad shape and the dimensions were poor, the lighting was bad, and there was no hitting background. But the people I felt most sorry for were those who had spent their money to see a major league exhibition. Believe me, there was no way a major league performance was going to be presented on the field we had to work with.

Still, the man the fans wanted to see most was The Hammer. And they did. They also got to see him hit a home run — a "shot" that must have traveled all of about 200 feet into the right field stands. Henry got jammed his first time up, swung in what could be considered self-defense and broke his bat in the bargain.

About the only good thing about such a game is that everyone usually gets in to play a couple of innings. Henry went 2 for 2, scored a run, had an RBI and then left the game for a pinch runner in the fourth inning. We were behind, 2-1, but came back in the seventh with four runs and won, 6-2.

Now, when I say that games like this let everybody on the club get in for an inning or two, I mean even the coaching staff. Once in a while the old war horses get the idea that they can still play, so we let them. In the Memphis game, third base coach Joe Nossek thought that he'd give it a try and pinch hit for pitcher Tom Hausman.

Joe really isn't very old — 35 — and was an active player in pro ball until 1971. The lucky son of a gun even played in the outfield for the 1965 Minnesota Twins and was in six games of that year's World

Series. So Joe was looking for his chance to show us just how things were to be done at the plate. After he found a bat he liked, finished fooling with the pine tar and digging into the batter's box, he drew a walk. Get 'em next time, Coach!

For Aaron, the game was a chance to visit with old friends on the Atlanta side of the field, and the experience might have broken some tensions for him.

Exhibition games like these during the season can, if organized properly, help keep a club loose and really ready to take on the world. But there are other things that can be done to keep things going in a positive way. Sometimes I don't think the fans are really aware of just how much idle time there is for ballplayers, especially on the road. With the schedules the way they are, some of this unproductive time is consumed by traveling from city to city, but there still is lots left over. It's during off-time that the mental outlook of a team can be shaped or shattered.

When you are on the road waiting to play a game, you can do only so much card playing and window shopping and television watching. With so many night games, we usually have time during the day to devote to other activities. Sometimes it's sleeping or reading the newspaper, but sometimes we need a little bit more activity to keep us going.

What we did to keep us from going off the deep end was have a regular meeting of our kangaroo court every Friday, home or away, rain or shine. The court turned out to be an important relaxer for our club, and most of us look forward to its continuation for a long time.

The guy who thought it would be a good idea for us was none other than Henry Louis Aaron. He said that the Braves used to have one, and that the Orioles had some fun with theirs. The idea sounded like a good one, and with that the officers were elected.

Our presiding judge early in the season was our Gold Glove first baseman, Hizzoner George C. Scott. We picked Boomer because we felt he'd be the best guy to handle the job, and also because he's a pretty funny guy. Judge Scott had two players who acted as his counselors — Aaron and Ed Sprague. It was their job to help determine fines and penalties. They also acted as aids in keeping the proceedings in proper legal order.

Any player could bring another player to trial. The guys up on charges were then able to pick other guys to help defend them. No one was immune, and all fines were payable immediately.

When court was in session, Scotty would sit at his bench fully outfitted in his judge's attire — a Brewers uniform, an English magistrate's powdered wig on his head and his baseball cap on top of that, worn in the turned-around style of a catcher. Boomer — excuse me, Judge Scott — would call the session to order, using a gavel he had made from one of his bats. The poor soul whose case was before the court would either approach the bench and plead guilty, or ask for a trial and take the witness stand.

As things go in daily life, where it is possible for even the most upstanding citizen to run afoul of the law, so things went in our baseball judicial system. Every player in the club was subject to facing charges, and when the laws were broken, the guilty had to pay.

Talking to the players from another team, even before the stadium gates were open, was a violation. That would cost the guilty party one buck in Judge Scott's courtroom. Better to pay the court than have one of the umpires catch you talking to the opposition after the gates had been opened. In that case, the League sees to it that your next paycheck is fifty dollars light.

You could also be taken to court if one of the guys on the club thought the last outfit you wore on the road left something to be desired in the matter of taste. You might have thought you looked fine, but if another guy thought you didn't, well . . . Good afternoon, Your Honor! And, brother, could the court be hard on you. If, in the opinion of the judge and his assistants, your choice of a particular shirt with a certain pair of slacks was not defended well enough by you or your attorney, another dollar went into the pot. If the court was in an angry mood, even one of the world's ten best dressed men would have had a hard time escaping a fine.

Shaving before a game has also been known to cost a buck, as has loitering in the training room enjoying a Coke — I know that penalty very well, since the court has fined me on that several times — or maybe even taking a little too long in the locker room to get ready for a game.

But most of all, the court was really fun, not only for the guys involved in the cases, but for us sitting in on the proceedings. A guy brought before the court could either plead guilty to the charge and pay his fine, or he could demand a full trial that included the acquiring of lawyers and witnesses. If a defendant won his case and was judged not guilty, he would go free and the plaintiff would have to pay. But if you asked for a trial and were found guilty, you had to pay double the normal fine, and the player you had as your defense lawyer also had to cough up.

One time the court fined every member of the club. We had worked out at home and had all worn our blue road uniforms, instead of our home whites. Everybody kicked in a dollar, and the court also fined the clubhouse man for putting out the wrong uniforms in our lockers.

Another time, we got on Boomer and fined him for not being able to carry out his duties on the bench. This all came about when Bill Castro was on the witness stand, preparing to testify in a case. As Bill sat down, Scotty turned away from the witness and began talking to Associate Judges Aaron and

Sprague. What he was doing, we found out in short order, was trying to get the witness' name. Forgetting a teammate's name cost George a dollar, and gave us all a big laugh.

The good thing about the court was that it got everyone on the team involved. Everybody took the court in a good mood, and even the coaches got a kick out of it, even though they all were brought before the judge from time to time.

If a guy got picked off first base, the court could just as easily levy a fine against the first base coach as it could against the guy who got nailed. The same thing would be true for a guy getting picked off third. And if a player got picked off second, the court would see to it that both Joe Nossek and Harvey Kuenn had chances to explain themselves, and add to the treasury.

Fines were issued for mental mistakes — getting picked off, pitchers not covering home or third, throwing the ball to the wrong base, not calling for pop flies — all were good for a dollar or more. But just as in the real world, we had some dandy cases of conspiracy that had to be tried, too.

One that comes to mind was a trial we had early in the season at Kansas City. Coach Joe Nossek filed charges against such cunning villains as Timmy Johnson, Mike Hegan, Kurt Bevacqua and the Billy the Kid of the bunch, Robin Yount. This dastardly crew perpetrated the most wicked of all crimes.

They took Joe's glove — if you want to call it a glove — and put all kinds of yucky stuff into it, including a goodly supply of tobacco juice. Joe was a little upset at that, even though some of the guys thought the operation on the delapidated antique made it look better. When the case was called, the four accused faced the bench and the evidence was placed before the panel of judges. Timmy picked up the glove, turned it inside out and poured red Kool-Aid into it. My roommate's idea was to show the court just how bad a glove Joe had.

Joe then took the stand to defend the honor of his glove. He told of the tradition and sentiment that were attached to his glove, and said that the damage done to it was a wanton act of cruel and unsportsmanlike conduct.

While the testimony was being given, the rest of us were sitting in the gallery, laughing at what had been done to the glove, and at the way Joe was milking every last ounce of sympathy out of his case. He put more feeling into his testimony than some of those actors do in the soap operas on daytime TV.

Finally, Nossek compared his glove and its meaning with the one our presiding judge used every day. That did it. Right then and there, the defendants lost all hope of winning their case. When Joe went into his routine about Scotty's glove, George's eyes lit up and you could almost see the guilty judgment forming on his lips. Boomer's glove is almost as bad as

Joe's. It has been sewn and patched so often that it looks like something out of Dr. Frankenstein's laboratory. But with his Black Magic — as Scotty calls his glove — there's not a better fielding first baseman in baseball.

He fined Timmy, Mike, Robin and Kurt two dollars each. And then, before he closed the case, he fined Timmy another dollar for pouring the Kool-Aid on the glove in the court's presence. That trial was one of the best all season.

One guy who seemed to be in court just about every time we had a session was Kurt Bevacqua. He was either before the judges as a witness, as a defendant or as a plaintiff. Surprisingly, he won most of his cases.

Honestly, though, the judgments of the court were pretty fair. When I look back over the season and see that the guy with the most money in the kitty was Hank Aaron — an associate judge and founder of the court — that proves to me that there was no political influence involved. But while the decisions against Aaron were fair, I think the fines against him were maybe a little excessive.

Henry was being fined just about every session. He'd go to court for fraternizing, lose and have to pay double. Another time he'd be brought up for doing something else wrong and ... wham! "Guilty!" It would cost Aaron another two or three dollars. I guess George felt that since Hank had it to pay, the court might as well get it while the getting was good.

The court was a good idea, though. Nobody ever came out of it with hard feelings, it kept the team loose, and made the players' relationships with the coaching staff easier. Every session was something to look forward to.

Chapter 7

The All~Star Game

If I had to use one word to describe the atmosphere surrounding the 1975 All-Star Game in Milwaukee on July 15, I'd have to select nostalgic.

Twenty years before, on July 12, 1955, the city of Milwaukee had played host for the first time to the midsummer exhibition between the best of the American and National Leagues. Back then, Milwaukee was the home of the Braves, the National League team that had moved from Boston in 1953. They played in the recently built Milwaukee County Stadium, the most modern baseball arena of the time. Since 1953 had marked the return of major league baseball to Milwaukee — the city was the home of one of the original clubs in the new American League in 1901 — the All-Star Game at the halfway point in the decade gave the Wisconsin city its first real chance to shine in baseball's national spotlight.

Baseball in those days was a simpler game, in some respects, than it is today. The two major leagues were made up of eight teams each, with no East and West Divisions, as we have in the twelve-team leagues now. The uniforms in those days were less spectacular and didn't look as trim as the ones we wear today. They were loose fitting and made of a wool flannel, but it was the dream of every kid who played baseball in my neighborhood in that era to one day slip into one of those suits, if only just for a minute. Almost every club had a basic white home uniform and a basic gray away suit. Some clubs wore pinstripes, but no one ever thought that bright blue, orange, green, yellow or even a suit of Hawaiian sunset hues, such as the Houston Astros wear, would ever take the place of the traditional subdued colors of the game.

But although the uniforms then weren't of the doubleknit variety, as ours are, the guys who filled them in the 1955 All-Star Game were some of the best ever to play ball. They came from Sportsman's Park in St. Louis, Crosley Field in Cincinnati, Forbes Field in Pittsburgh, Connie Mack Stadium in Philadelphia and from Mr. Phil Wrigley's park in Chicago, where he held firm to his belief that baseball was a game to be played only in the light of God's sunshine.

The 1975 Stars from those towns played in Busch Stadium, Riverfront Stadium, Three Rivers Stadium, Veterans Stadium, and, yes, Mr. Wrigley's still day-game-only ballpark.

In midsummer of 1955, though, the eyes of the baseball world were on the two year old, five million dollar home of the Milwaukee Braves.

On the American League lineup card that afternoon were the names of such men as the Red Sox' Ted Williams; Yankees' Mickey Mantle, Yogi Berra and Whitey Ford; Detroit's Al Kaline; Cleveland pitching ace Early Wynn; Al Rosen . . . Chico Carrasquel . . . Nellie Fox . . . Bobby Avila . . . Mickey Vernon . . . Billy Pierce . . . Jackie Jensen . . . Vic Power . . . Frank Sullivan . . . and a local Wisconsin boy, Harvey Kuenn.

Although he was on the American League side of the field, our batting coach must have been one of the most popular men on the field that day. Born in Milwaukee, Harvey had starred in football, basketball and baseball at a local high school before going on to the University of Wisconsin. He signed to play in the majors with the Detroit Tigers in 1952, was the American League Rookie of the Year in 1953, and played for 14 years in the big leagues. Harvey, who won the American League's batting title in 1959 with a .353 average in a Tiger uniform, was playing in his second All-Star Game in '55 and took the field as a shortstop. When his career was through, he had played in seven All-Star Games, had been in the World Series with the San Francisco Giants, and had compiled a lifetime major league batting average of .303.

For the Nationals, the lineup was just as strong. Red Schoendienst was still with the Cardinals then, although in just a couple of years he would be with the Braves and help them win two pennants. The Phillies were represented by Robin Roberts, Del Ennis and Stan Lopata. Don Newcombe was there from the Dodgers. Ernie Banks of the Cubs was playing in his first All-Star Game. And there were the great Stan Musial, Duke Snider, Willie Mays playing in his second of 24 All-Star Games, big Ted Kluszewski . . . Don Mueller . . . Smoky Burgess . . . Frank Thomas . . . Harvey Haddix . . . Gil Hodges . . . Gene Baker . . . Willie Jones . . . Joe Nuxhall . . . and the representatives from the hometown Braves.

Playing at third base that day for the Nationals was one of the most popular men to ever play in Milwaukee, Eddie Mathews. The pitcher who got credit for the win — he struck out all three American Leaguers he faced in the twelfth inning — was hometown favorite Gene Conley. Shortstop Johnny Logan went 1 for 3 that day, had an RBI as well and recorded a putout and an assist. The two other Braves who played that day were appearing in their first All-Star

Game. One was catcher Del Crandall. The other was right fielder Henry Aaron!

The game was one of the most exciting in the history of All-Star play. The Nationals, down 5-0 after six innings, scored two runs in the seventh and three in the eighth to tie the game and send it into extra innings. Stan Musial then led off the bottom of the twelfth with a home run into the right field bleachers to give the Nationals a 6-5 victory.

Hank Aaron, the youngest member of the winning squad at 21, had a good day at the plate in 1955. Although he didn't get into the game until the fifth inning, when he ran for Mueller, he had two hits, a run batted in, a run scored and a walk. Who could have known then that twenty years later, Aaron would still be an All-Star?

I don't remember very much about that 1955 game myself, but being in Milwaukee just before the 1975 game made it easy to become versed in what had happened. Just about every television station and newspaper carried something about the '55 game, as well as what would be going on at County Stadium the night of July 15. Interviews with former ballplayers and pictures from the 1955 All-Star show filled some part of each day's media coverage. There also seemed to be a definite effort by the people in Milwaukee to remember what had gone before and to get into the spirit of what was about to take place.

Workouts and a news conference were scheduled

for the teams on Monday, and before the game on Tuesday, the players, baseball officials and many fans attended an All-Star luncheon in MECCA, the convention and entertainment center downtown. Sharon went to the All-Star luncheon with some of the other Brewer wives as guests of the club while I stayed back at our hotel and watched our kids.

After the luncheon, I learned from Sharon that the pot roast served wasn't bad, and the rest of the program was great. Henry Aaron was the representative of all the players on the two squads and was given the symbolic first All-Star ring. Rod Carew was then called forward and received the Gillette Award for being the player who accumulated the most votes from the fans. The Twins second baseman had over 3.2 million ballots cast for him out of a total vote of 7.3 million.

The next man to step to the platform was former Brave manager Fred Haney. The skipper of the World Champion Milwaukee Braves of 1957 and National League Champs for 1958 accepted a check for $10,000 to be presented to the Baseball Players Association of America for our pension fund.

Houston Astro first baseman Bob Watson was next on the list of those to be called forward as he was given a watch by The Tootsie Roll Company to memorialize his scoring of the one-millionth run in the history of major league baseball. Dave Concepcion of the Reds also got a watch for just missing that feat!

Say, if they are going to do that, maybe somebody ought to think about giving Chris Chambliss something. He, too, just missed the honor in New York when we played the Yankees on May 4, when Boomer cut him down at home on a really great play.

Another presentation was made to Henry, a gift from the other side of the world. Sadaharu Oh, the home run king of Japanese baseball, had sent an autographed gold cap to the Home Run King of all of baseball.

The game, of course, had been sold out for weeks and the new seats that had been installed allowed a County Stadium record crowd of 51,480 to attend the game. That was better than 6,000 more than had attended the 1955 game.

Since I wasn't playing, I went to watch, along with my wife, Sharon, and our two youngsters. We sat along the first base line in an area with a lot of other players and their families. For those who are interested, the ballplayers have to pay for their tickets!

The field looked like a brand new diamond. Earlier in the season, two popular rock music groups, the Rolling Stones and Pink Floyd, had given concerts at the stadium just a couple of weeks apart, and the thousands of rock fans trampled the turf. Then we ran into a rainy spell, and the groundskeepers could hardly get the field in shape for play. Something had to be done, and that meant resodding.

That resodding of the infield and parts of the outfield began right after our night game with the Red

Sox on July 3, just before we went on the road. As I left the locker room, I noticed that the lights were still on inside the stadium. I walked up one of the ramps and saw that the grounds crew had already begun getting the field ready for the All-Star Game.

There were guys with front end loaders cutting out the dead grass and preparing the soil to take on a fresh layer of sod. When we returned from the trip for a three game series with the White Sox just before the All-Star break, the entire infield and parts of the outfield had been replaced with new sod and attended to. Some of the patches hadn't grown in as they should have, and there were still some brown spots, but a little green dye took care of those areas.

So, there were a couple of players from the National League who had some comments to make about how bad an infield we had. They should have seen it in June! And if they'd like to come over some time in September and see what it's like after the Packers have churned up the place — third base is right on one of the goal lines and plays like sand on a beach in the late weeks of the season — they are more than welcome to try.

At any rate, County Stadium was ready for the All-Star Game. And so was Hank Aaron, who had come full circle in his career as a major leaguer. Twenty years after his first All-Star game in Milwaukee as a member of the Braves, he was back to play his second All-Star game in County Stadium and his first as an American Leaguer.

Aaron was the most called-out-to player from either club. Fans looked for him to come near the rails, and whenever a player wearing a blue cap emerged from the dugout, they waited expectantly for him. Photographers followed his moves on the field, almost as if in a replay of our home opener.

Although I didn't deserve selection to the '75 game, it was the one game that I really wanted to be a part of. I believe that if you polled all the Brewers that night, they would have responded in the same way, simply because the game was being played in our home park. Being on an All-Star squad is great, but when you can be an All-Star and play in front of the fans who watch you for 81 games a season, that makes it all the more special. I know that George Scott's idea when he got into the game was to hit one out of the park for the fans. He felt that hitting a home run in an All-Star game before a Milwaukee crowd would have been the greatest way to say thanks to the many people who supported him and the club. Most assuredly, he was disappointed when he struck out twice.

Not being in the game allowed me to do something that I don't often do — and that's sit with my family and watch a baseball game. I knew that Sharon enjoyed the play as it was her first time at an All-Star performance. On the other hand, Donald and Shannon just thought it was another ball game and left it at that. But for me, sitting with my family in the stands was a real treat.

There were two things about the pageantry that I especially liked. The first was the designation of honorary team captains for each club. On the far side of the field, the National Leaguers had Stan Musial in their dugout. Among the American Leaguers on the first base side was Mickey Mantle. Both Hall of Famers had been in the 1955 All-Star Game and their presence added a bit of color and nostalgia to the show.

The other thing was having Secretary of State Henry Kissinger throw out the first ball. Dr. Kissinger's first sports love is soccer, but he also professes to be a real baseball fan. He followed the Yankees as a youngster in New York City, then switched his allegiance to the Red Sox while teaching at Harvard. Having the Secretary of State throw out the first ball really added something to the program.

National League Manager Walter Alston of the 1974 Champion Dodgers and his players were brought out first, starting players individually, then the alternates and coaches as a group. Two of the National Leaguers were making their second appearances in an All-Star Game in Milwaukee, but this time they were not performing as players. One, of course, was the hero of the 1955 game, Honorary Captain Stan Musial. The other was Red Schoendienst, the present manager of the Cardinals and the National League's third base coach, who played second base in '55. Besides Aaron and Mantle on the

American League team, there was another who had played in the '55 game — our manager, Del Crandell, who had been the National League catcher. Del was the third base coach this time.

The American League All-Stars were introduced, and after the starters had been welcomed, the rest of the players lined up on the foul line going down toward first base. The names of the substitute players were called out until, finally: "From the Milwaukee Brewers . . . (loud applause) . . . Henry Aaron . . . . ."

The words had hardly been spoken when the crowd sprang to a standing ovation. George Scott also got a nice round of applause when his name was called next, but that was about three minutes later, after temporary suspension of the introductions was required to let Hank's ovation die down.

Glen Campbell sang the national anthem, Dr. Kissinger threw out the first ball, the American League starters took the field, and the 1975 All-Star Game was underway.

Vida Blue of the Oakland A's, the last winning pitcher for the Americans, in 1971, started and had no trouble until the second inning, when he gave up consecutive home runs to Dodgers Steve Garvey and Jimmy Wynn. Wynn's solo shot into the left field stands made a little bit of history, since it was the 100th home run hit in All-Star play. And the consecutive homers marked only the third time that such a feat had been accomplished. Al Rosen and Ray Boone did it first in the 1954 game and Ted Williams and Mickey Mantle did it again two years later.

There were no runs scored in the home half of the second, but another record was tied when pinch hitting Hank Aaron made his 24th All-Star appearance. Actually, Aaron had been an All-Star every year since 1955 and would have tied the record held by Musial and Willie Mays in 1974 had it not been for an ankle injury that kept him out of the first game in 1962. For four years, 1959, '60, '61 and '62, there were two All-Star Games each season. So Hank actually was a member of 25 All-Star teams.

When Henry stepped out of the dugout to bat for Blue, he got another standing ovation. There were two outs, with Gene Tenace of the A's on second and his Oakland teammate, Campy Campaneris, on first. Hank gave it a real try, taking a good cut at Pirate Jerry Reuss' first pitch. Unfortunately, he lined a hard, broken bat drive to Dave Concepcion for the final out of the inning. And for Henry Aaron in his 24th appearance in an All-Star Game, that was it.

That really wasn't too surprising. Like many other great stars, he has not had the best of luck in the All-Star Game. Through 1975, Henry has had only 13 hits in 67 times at bat for a lifetime All-Star Game average of just .194. He has scored seven runs, stolen two bases, driven in eight runs, and hit just two home runs.

Yet, in the games that really count, Hank has been spectacular. I know lots of players who would trade one of their good years for one of Henry's bad ones.

The game moved on until the bottom of the sixth, when Boston's Carl Yastrzemski hit a pinch three run homer to tie the score, 3-3. Yaz hit the ball better than 400 feet into the bullpen in right center field for his first homer as an All-Star. He also was the first to hit a homer off the Mets' Tom Seaver in Seaver's five appearances for the National League.

The National League added three more runs in the top of the ninth. Cardinal Reggie Smith opened the inning with a looper to left center, and when Claudell Washington of the A's misjudged it, the ball dropped in for a hit. And if things weren't bad enough for the 20-year-old Washington, they got worse when Al Oliver of the Pirates sliced a drive to left that bounced crazily off the fence and gave the National League two base runners.

Manager Alvin Dark called time and replaced Catfish Hunter with White Sox right hander Rich Gossage. Gossage, who had recorded 73 strikeouts in 80 innings during the first half of the season, was called in to get a very much needed strikeout. Instead, Rich cut loose with a pitch that nicked Larry Bowa of the Phillies and loaded the bases for the National League. Bill Madlock then pulled a change-up down the third base line, past Graig Nettles, and the visiting Nationals got two more runs.

Washington's throw to the plate got past Tenace for an error on the catcher, and then Gossage, who was backing up the play at home, tried to throw Bowa out at third but instead hit third base coach Red Schoendienst with the ball. Bowa scored the final run of the game on Pete Rose's sacrifice fly.

In the bottom of the ninth, the American League went down in order, and the National League won its 12th game in the last 13, 6-3.

The game wasn't a bad one, though, and it appeared that the fans had enjoyed it, even though the American League lost.

When the game was over, it was announced that the most valuable player award would be shared by two members of the winning side, Bill Madlock of the Chicago Cubs and Jon Matlack of the New York Mets. Madlock's two run base hit in the ninth inning broke the 3-3 tie and was probably the biggest hit of the game. Matlack, the pitcher who got credit for the win, worked the seventh and eighth innings, gave up just two hits and struck out four.

In the clubhouse later, one of the writers asked Aaron if 1975 would be his last year as a player. Hank gave no definite answer. "If this is my last All-Star Game, it's nice to have it come in the city where I played my first," he said.

One player who could have played in his first Milwaukee All-Star Game didn't. Cleveland's Buddy Bell disqualified himself. He didn't think his play was of all star caliber! And to me, that decision alone proves he is an all star.

Chapter 8

The Man and The Athlete

After a great start, the 1975 baseball season turned out poorly for the Milwaukee Brewers. We slumped badly after the All-Star Game and although we closed out the campaign by winning our last four games, our season record was only 68-94. Our winning average of .420 was much lower than the .500 I had figured us for. For most of the last half of the season we were not in the division race. The Boston Red Sox won in the American League East, finishing four games ahead of the fast closing Orioles and 28 games ahead of us. Our low finish was our own fault. When you are at the bottom of the league in both team batting and pitching, you can't blame a bad year on anything else.

One of the first questions that comes to mind, though, pertains to Hank Aaron and the role our designated hitter played. How much did Henry Aaron help the Milwaukee Brewers in 1975? For me, that's an easy question to answer.

On the field, Aaron didn't have the year he expected. His .234 batting average, 12 home runs and 60 RBI's were far below the totals Henry thought he would come up with in his first season in the American League. I'm sure he would be the first to admit that, as a designated hitter, he just wasn't effective.

He did, however, help the club in other ways. The evidence may not stand out in bold letters, but just having him in the lineup added much to the modest success we did at times achieve. The players batting ahead of and behind him got better selections of pitches, just because Henry still was a threat with a bat in his hands. The opposing pitchers really thought about how they would pitch to him. They didn't want to take a chance, then lose the game because they had underestimated him.

Early in the season, Henry hit the ball fairly well, even though he didn't get too many hits. He was making contact and keeping the guys on the mound off balance. What caused Aaron most of his troubles was just getting used to the American League style of pitching after all his years in the National League. Aaron saw a lot of breaking balls every time he stepped to the plate, and nobody really challenged his power until late in the season. Whenever you

"I can imagine . . . Henry was reflecting on the good memories he had from his years in Milwaukee with the Braves — memories that are fond and warm and deeply satisfying." (Pg. 38)

"I was struck by his appearance the first time I saw him in a Brewer uniform. I just couldn't stop thinking that the man wearing Number 44 was the greatest home run hitter in the history of baseball." (Pg. 47)

"He worked on his swing until it sounded as though a machine, instead of a man were rapping baseballs. . . into the outfield and often over the fence."
(Pg. 50)

*"His style and dedication were evident
— nothing flashy, but he worked hard to
get ready to do what he does best."*
(Pg. 51)

"George Scott, our resident slugger . . .
felt that by hitting behind Aaron, he
would get better pitches and less
pressure. George came to camp $750
overweight, but he had always been one
of the hardest workers in the Spring."
(Pg. 49)

*"The club dropped its policy against
mustaches. About 80% of us left Arizona
with something growing on our upper
lips . . . the new growth looked better on
some (Porter) than on others." (Pg. 59)*

"The first thing Aaron asked me about was if any of the guys played golf. Not long afterward . . . we went out as a team and the ice was broken with the veterans." (Pg. 48)

"Aaron's presentation was at the request of Del Crandall. The hitting clinic dealt mainly with little tips on batting. Hearing them from Aaron made a difference . . . Aaron is the proof of the rule and the example to follow." (Pgs. 54-56)

"Henry asked the crowd of newsmen surrounding his locker: 'And go talk to Billy Champion. He pitched a fine game. We've got a fine young team here. I just want to be a part of it.'" (Pg. 72)

For a power hitter, Aaron has always been a pretty fair base runner. He is one of only five players to hit 30 home runs and steal 30 bases in one season (44 homers, 31 steals, '63). He has also hit 98 triples! This sequence shows a young Aaron caught trying to stretch one of those into an inside-the-park homer against the Dodgers.

"When it was cold, Henry kept his
batting helmet on all the time, and went
directly into the batter's box . . . when it
got warmer, Aaron carried his bat and
his helmet to the home plate area."
(Pg. 84)

"When you're on the road, waiting to play a game, you can do only so much card playing and window shopping and television watching." Author Money takes a moment to write to his family.

"When court was in session, Scotty
would sit at his bench fully outfitted in
his judge's attire — a Brewers uniform,
an English magistrate's powdered wig
and his baseball cap. We felt he'd be the
best guy to handle the job and he's a
pretty funny guy." (Pg. 101)

"One guy who seemed to be in court just about every time was Kurt Bevacqua." Bevacqua, Number 2, checks his "swing" with Gorman Thomas during pre-season shenanigans. (Pg. 106)

"July 12, 1955, the City of Milwaukee
played host for the first time to the All-
Star Game." That's Willie Mays taking a
home run away from someone. (Pg. 114)

*"Playing at third base that day for the
Nationals was one of the most popular
men to ever play in Milwaukee,
Eddie Mathews." (Pg. 114)*

"*Hank said he had been fortunate to play most of his career with good hitting clubs. The guys batting around you in the line up have a lot to do with your own performance at the plate.*" Eddie Mathews made his home run trot ahead of Aaron hundreds of times. (Pg. 75)

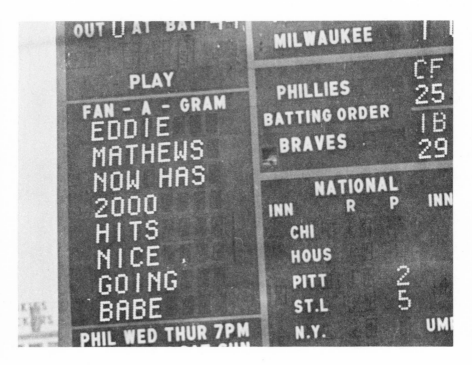

There was a time when many fans expected Eddie Mathews to challenge Ruth's records. Note that the scoreboard even gave him an occasional salute with Ruth's nickname.

*"Born in Milwaukee, Harvey Kuenn . . .
was playing in his second All-Star
Game in '55 and took the field as a
shortstop." (Pg. 113)*

This man was one of five hometown
favorites playing in the 1955 classic. Del
Crandall was joined by Mathews,
Aaron, shortstop Johnny Logan and
pitcher Gene Conley. (Pg. 114)

Even a major league family has difficulty getting two impish children to sit still long enough for a family album candid! Don Money and his wife Sharon might not know it, but Donald, Jr. is already optioned to the Brewers and Shannon has her bid in as "Bonnie Brewer" for 1986!

In his hometown of Vineland, New
Jersey, author Money shares off-season
broadcasting duties for high school
sports with friend Herb Anastor (left).
Don shows one of his souvenir bats to
Anastor who worked with him on the
manuscript for *The Man Who Made
Milwaukee Famous.*

"Boomer showed all season why he was our most valuable player. He finished with a .285 batting average, led the league in RBI's with 109, had 176 hits and tied for the league lead in home runs with 36." (Pg. 175)

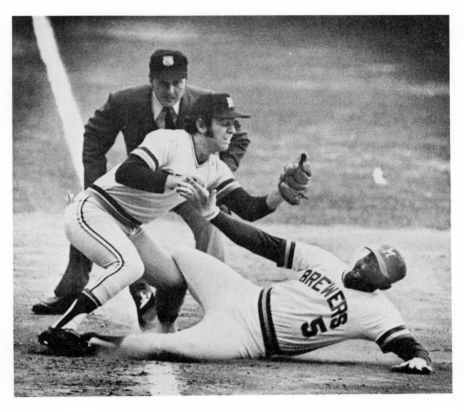

*"Boomer plays to win. Scott finished the
season just as if we had been in a race to
the wire. He proved himself to be the
team leader he was selected to be."*
(Pg. 177)

"Hank Aaron has mentioned, more than
a couple of times, that Yount has what it
takes. He was named the American
League's player of the month for April in
1975. At the time, he was still 19, the
youngest player to ever receive that
honor." (Pg. 180)

*"Probably the most underrated ball
player on the squad, Charlie Moore did
a lot to find a place in our line up."*
(Pg. 182)

An enthusiastic bench can help win
many games.

You be the judge! See page 134 for another view of the Brewers' Darrel Porter, hands-down winner of the best mustache award on the '75 squad.

*"I thought Del did a pretty good job with
the Brewers. The manager . . . probably
gets more than his share of the blame."*
(Pg. 190)

"I think our club is rough on a manager, because we have so many young ball players." (Pg. 189)

Now starting his eighth year as a major
league third baseman, Money already
holds five Major League records for
fielding.

change leagues, it takes about a season to get adjusted to the differences.

Henry certainly was not pleased with his season. Even though he was playing in the twilight of his career, he still wanted to do the job. We talked from time to time about hitting and some of the pitchers in the league, and it was easy to see that he was disgusted with his batting. He went through real anguish after games in which he went 0 for 4 and maybe, at best, hit a couple of weak ground balls that barely got out of the infield. He wasn't disgusted by his lack of home runs, but he did feel that he should have been able to hit better than the lower .230's.

But he didn't, for even an instant, have a give-up attitude. I feel, though, that he did show his age and difficulty in adjusting to an entirely new situation. Perhaps one American League season just wasn't enough for him to get acclimated. This seems especially true to me, realizing that for all but one or two games Hank sat on the bench between times at bat. Those prolonged periods of inactivity might have kept him from really getting into the swing of things.

After the year that he had in 1974, when he hit 20 home runs and broke the Babe's mark but had only a .268 batting average, I think his pride made him want to prove that he could still do the job. And even with his low average in 1975, his career mark at the end of the season still was an admirable .307. I think that if he had the same choice to make over again, he'd do the same thing. In fact, he is coming back for one more shot in 1976. Good for Hank, and good for the Brewers.

In the dugout, Hank's a quiet guy. But then, when you're sitting in the dugout, trying to concentrate on the game, nobody says much. It's just not the time or place. After the game, Henry might sometimes have given a helpful hint to another player, but he wasn't the type who made those suggestions just because he had hit all those home runs. Mostly, unless he was asked to say something, he kept quiet and let the coaches and manager run the ball club.

In the locker room, it was another story. Aaron was loose and got along well with everybody. He didn't hang around with one particular crowd, he liked a good joke, and he did put a lot of money into the Kangaroo Court kitty. That helped make the party with the court's treasury money a real success.

Certainly, Hank did not hurt the club in any way. If we had had another DH capable of hitting .260 or .270 who was being kept out of the lineup, that would have been a different story. But since the DH rule has been in effect, the Brewers have not had a designated hitter able to produce in that area. So, although we didn't improve, we didn't lose anything, either. Hank helped just by being around some of the younger players — myself included. His understanding of hitting is immense, and if you ask, he will give you a hand. He's a very easy guy to get along with, expects to be treated no better or worse than the rest of the players, and takes things just as they come.

His popularity with the fans was tremendous, both on the road and at home, and I think he had a lot to do with a change in the size and makeup of our home crowds. I noticed more older fans at our games — people who remembered Aaron back in the days of the Braves. And there were more younger fans, too — those who had only heard of him and wanted to see him in action before he called it a career. There was real love for this man pouring out of the stands wherever we went. I saw no signs of the animosity he sometimes experienced when he was going after Ruth's record in the National League. He was really well received.

Off the field, Hank Aaron took care of his appearances for the Magnavox television company, and attended luncheons in his honor almost all over the country. But he never neglected his responsibilities to the team. If we had to be at the park at a certain time, Henry was there with the rest of us. He took care of what he was able to, but only until it threatened his baseball. That, to him, was always first.

When we played at home, we didn't see much of Henry after the games. He tried to get away from the hustle and bustle and I really can't blame him. He helped out the club whenever possible with publicity, but like the rest of us who spend a good portion of our year away from home, he liked to have free time to do things on his own.

It was a little different on the road. He often went out with a bunch of us for dinner and maybe a couple of beers in some quiet place before getting back to the hotel. We'd sit in the back of the restaurant, where it was quiet and a bit private, and talk and joke and just have a good time. And after going out with Hank just once, the thought of who he was never went beyond the point that identified him as just another teammate. And he never did anything to make us feel any other way.

No matter how hard we tried to stay unnoticed, though, there was always someone who realized that our group included Henry Aaron. People would come up to him to talk and get his autograph. That made it a little hard for us sometimes to get away from the game. Henry also ran into lots of fans when we flew from one city to another. People would recognize him in the airports, and if we had to take a regular commercial flight, instead of a charter, the requests for autographs sometimes got to be just too much. He would have to ask a stewardess to stop the steady stream. He never minded signing autographs and meeting the fans when he was able to, but attending to the needs of 150 people on an airplane was a bit more than he could handle. It is hard to be "on" all the time, but I think people who have seen Aaron deal with fans will admit that he does more than his share.

The club tried to relieve Aaron of some of that crush. In some parks, where it was possible, he would leave the locker room by a different exit and go back to the hotel by private car. Or, he would be the last one out of the locker room so that once he got on the bus, we could leave for the hotel or airport right away. Even so, Hammer wound up signing an awful lot of autographs. There may be some disappointed fans somewhere, but I don't know of any occasion when Hank Aaron ever refused to honor a courteous autograph request.

Hotel security was also a bit different for him. Usually, if someone knows a player and wants to get through to him at his hotel, it's not hard to get the call through. There is some screening of calls, since the club, as well as the hotels, don't want us bothered at all hours of the day or night by fans who just want to chat. But ballplayers are not an unreachable group. In Aaron's case, though, the register usually had him listed under another name. That kept his whereabouts from the public, and also made it easier for him to order room or valet service without having to sign a dozen balls for the hotel staff. Such precautions often are necessary to allow Hank some peace and quiet.

Having played more than twenty years in the big leagues, Aaron has adjusted to public life very well. His baseball career has been fabulous, and he is assured a place in the Baseball Hall of Fame. But where does he go from here?

That was a big question when Del Crandall was fired shortly before our disappointing season ended. With Crandall gone, would Henry become the new manager? Would he play ball another year after a poor showing in '75? Would business offers take Aaron away from the game?

Those questions were answered in a joint statement issued by Hank and club officials November 6. Yes, Henry would play his last year of his two year contract, then retire to a vice-presidency in the Brewers' front office. On the very next day, the Brewers announced that they had selected Alex Grammas, the third base coach of the World Series winning Cincinnati Reds, to manage the team for the next three seasons.

I was really kind of surprised that Hank had chosen to play his second year. Besides not having done well in '75, he had been offered several business opportunities. I figured that he probably would take the manager's job with the Brewers, or retire from baseball altogether and take the beer distributorship he supposedly had been offered. But then when he announced his decision to return for another year, I thought to myself, "Yeah, that's the only way Henry would ever go out."

Being close to him as a teammate, I've come to know that Hank is the kind of guy who wants to go out on top, or, at least have a chance to go out on top. He could have done that at the end of the '74 season, but he still wanted to play. Now, after an unsatisfactory '75 season, I think he wants to go out and play another year just to prove that he still can do it and that he wasn't just hanging on. If he hits .275 or better in his last year, I think he will have shown he hasn't lost his touch, that it was just adjusting to a new league that gave him a little trouble. Even if he has a bad year, all it will prove is that a great player hung on just a little too long. It certainly won't take anything away from what he has done.

With Alex becoming our manager, there has been talk that Aaron was passed over. My understanding is that Henry was offered the job in September, while Del was still running the club, and that he turned it down because of his long friendship with Del. He didn't want to be the guy who would come in and knock his old friend out of the box. Still, I really don't think that Henry Aaron has forgotten about being a manager in the big leagues. I just think many things made it the wrong time for him to take on that kind of responsibility.

The 1976 season could be one of Henry's best ever. It being his last, I think he'll just go out and hit as only he can hit, and that'll be it.

I don't think his position on the club will change much with Alex the manager, either. Hank certainly won't be as close to Alex as he was to Del, but I will be very much surprised if Alex doesn't make some use of Aaron's talents as a part time instructor, just as Del did. And I think Hank will be more than willing to do whatever he can to help the ball club. Aaron is just that kind of guy.

I must admit that I was surprised when the Brewers hired Grammas. I had sort of expected it would be Gene Mauch, who not only is an experienced field manager but was available, besides. But according to Jim Baumer, our general manager, the hiring of Alex could be the single most important thing the Brewers have done since they set up shop in Milwaukee in 1970. I don't know Alex very well, but Jim may well be right on target with that outlook.

I had my only real association with Alex Grammas in the National League, when I was playing with the Phillies and he was coaching with the Reds. He joined the Reds in 1970, after having been a coach for five years with the Pittsburgh Pirates. His playing career spanned 15 years, 10 as a major league infielder with the Cardinals, Reds and Cubs. When he was coaching third base for the Reds, he was acknowledged as Manager Sparky Anderson's right hand man.

As a manager, he may be completely different. In fact, I expect that his outlook will be much different when it comes to dealing with ballplayers now. More and different responsibilities almost certainly require such a change, and if what he said when he was hired in November holds true during the season, Alex will run a tight and uniform ship.

Alex said that he wanted to instill a winning attitude in the squad and bring back a level of confidence we seemed to have for only parts of each of the last few seasons. He also said that everyone in a Milwaukee uniform would be treated alike. In the past, we've had some players who have either been more equal than others, or who haven't done all they should have because of special treatment by some in the front office. Alex or any man in charge on the field can really do only as much as the club will let him. If he doesn't get the support of the front office, all his good intentions will be worth little. If he doesn't have full authority on the field, his effectiveness with the players will be less than acceptable.

I think to get the Brewers going real well in '76, there will have to be some trades made to get more depth and body to the lineup. When you look at our regular starting lineup from '75, you can't help but notice that we were a very young club. Only Boomer and myself, among the regulars, had more than three years of big league experience. That kind of lineup is a tough one to win with. Playing with so many young-sters on a club also doesn't give you much bench strength. To do well in a pennant race, you need some older players who have been through it all before. They may not be able to play every day, but they will be able to fill in when needed and not cause you to lose ground.

The Brewers also need to try for some established pitchers, and maybe an outfielder or two. The 1976 Brewers will have at least two guys back from 1975, Robin Yount and Henry Aaron. They really are the club's only untouchables — Robin because of his fantastic potential and Henry because he has chosen to spend the last year of his illustrious career in Milwaukee.

Once Henry's playing career is over and he

becomes an active vice-president, I think many more opportunities will open for him. But I think, too, that his most able contributions will be in his work with the club. Certainly some of his responsibilities as a club official will keep him active in the instructional part of the game. It would be terribly difficult to keep Aaron away from the balls and bats once the doors to spring training camp open. As an executive, he will have just as much to offer to the organization and the game, especially with the young players coming up.

My relationship with Aaron as a teammate was a good one, and I hope it will continue for many years. I have found him to be an easy and comfortable man, more than just a sports personality of great skill and ability.

He is a quiet guy who doesn't show much emotion. If he doesn't like a call, he talks to the umpires a bit, just as we all do. But he won't go much beyond that. He is not a helmet thrower or a water cooler kicker. When he is angry at himself for taking a called third strike or popping a pitch to the first baseman, Aaron returns to the dugout, hangs his helmet on its hook and puts his cap back on, all without any unusual carrying on. But the look of frustration is definitely on his face.

Is there anything bad about the man? Not that I can see. And there is nothing about him that I would be hesitant or embarrassed to tell anyone. He enjoys a beer after the game, or an occasional cigarette, but he certainly doesn't overdo those things. He makes a lot of public appearances for the club and gives of himself 100% when he's meeting the fans. He gets paid for some of those appearances, but he could just as well say he doesn't want to do them. That, though, is not his nature. Just by being Hank Aaron, he does a lot for all of us in baseball.

I'm glad I had the opportunity to play with Henry Aaron. I had heard and read about the way he handled himself, but seeing it firsthand made an even greater impression on me. I wouldn't have given up the chance to be his teammate for anything. That alone made 1975, for me, just a super year.

But I guess the best thing I can say about Henry Aaron is this: Athletic achievements or not, if my son wanted to pattern himself after The Hammer, I couldn't think of a better man for him to follow.

Chapter 9

Some Other Brewers

Although the main emphasis of this book is on Henry Aaron, from the viewpoint of another ballplayer, obviously, Hank Aaron is not all there is to the ball club. And despite the team's disappointing season in 1975, there were some players who had a good season as individuals.

The first guy who comes to mind is our first baseman, **George Scott**. Boomer showed all season why he was our most valuable player. He finished with a .285 batting average, led the league in RBI's with 109, had 176 hits and tied for the league lead in home runs with Reggie Jackson of the A's, each hitting 36. He also had another fine year at the bag, and took very seriously his role as the first team captain in Milwaukee Brewer history.

Just to show how young a club we were, George turned 31 during spring training and he was the oldest of the regulars.

A football, basketball and baseball star in his hometown of Greenville, Mississippi, Boomer signed with the Boston Red Sox in 1962 and moved through the Red Sox minor league chain steadily. He was most valuable player in the Eastern League in 1965, and joined the Red Sox in 1966. As a rookie, he tied a major league record by playing in all 162 games and was an alternate on the American League All-Star team. He was traded to the Brewers in 1972 and won a Gold Glove for his fielding. It was his fourth, and he has kept on winning them ever since. Scott is one of the few guys on the roster who has played in a World Series.

That's the record book stuff on George Scott. There is a lot more to Scotty than that, though.

Boomer was named team captain not long after the season began. Del told us that George deserved the honor because he had had a good year every year, and was a veteran who would be able to work with some of the younger guys.

I think Boomer was a good choice, the logical man for the job. Not everybody thought that way, though. He was respected by some of the guys, but was poorly received by a few others. Some of the younger guys just wouldn't listen to him or Crandall. When I came up to the big leagues and an older player took me aside to give me pointers about hitting, fielding, running the bases or whatever, I was glad someone was taking an interest and I listened. But today, some of the younger guys don't want to be bothered. If you try to help them, they just don't want to hear it.

On the field, Boomer plays to win. Between innings, when he throws the ball around the infield, George's easy manner belies the fact that he is very intense — not only about the game but about the way he will play it. We certainly had our share of problems in 1975, and it would have been easy for a guy to just go through the motions and pack it in until the next year, but Boomer finished the season just as if we had been in a race to the wire. He proved himself to be the team leader he was selected to be.

George is also one of our most flamboyant players. Swinging a 40 ounce bat and wearing a necklace of what he describes as second basemen's teeth, Scotty gets a lot of ink when it comes to the color part of the game. He is one of the best dressers in the big leagues. He has all kinds of suits, shoes and shirts that he can mix and match, and he really looks good when we go on the road. The first $100,000 a year ballplayer on the club, he also enjoys motoring around town in a Continental Mark IV with the word "Boomer" on the bumper. George Scott has a good time being George Scott!

Surprisingly, though, George is kind of a loner. He

is popular with most of the players, relates to the fans well and is definitely a funny guy. But when we're on the road, Scotty usually stays to himself. He doesn't drink at all, so if a bunch of us decide to go out and have a beer after the game, you won't find him in the group. Often, he takes in a movie if he has some time before the game. Afterward, he usually goes back to his hotel room, orders room service and watches TV. He does have one special friend, though. He is Reggie Jackson's hitting guru, and every time we play the A's, you can see the two of them standing in the outfield talking about hitting, hitting, and more hitting. If one happens to be in a slump, he will get on the phone to the other.

As the judge of our kangaroo court, George did a good job. We had the court until the last two or three weeks of the season, although for the final part of the year, the man in charge was not our first baseman.

When Scotty was named captain, some of the guys thought that he shouldn't be both judge and captain, so we elected someone else to fill the vacant seat. Of the original group of judges, only Aaron remained in office at season's end. When Eddie Sprague's knee operation took him out of the lineup, Mike Hegan took over, and when George bowed out because of his new duties, Tom Murphy joined the panel as the third judge.

But no matter what his role on the field, in the dugout or in the locker room, George Scott was an important part of our ball club. He was always ready to play.

Another guy with that kind of attitude — even though he did have his troubles in '75 — was our kid shortstop, **Robin Yount**.

When he made our club in 1974, at 18, he became the youngest regular in the big leagues. He had only two months of pro experience behind him, but made the big move from Class A minor league ball to the big time with poise well beyond his years.

One thing to keep in mind about Robin Yount and his career is that he has not had the luxury of making mistakes down in the minor leagues. He has had to learn to play his position under fire against the best ballplayers in the game. He didn't learn his craft against guys his own age, but instead has faced the toughest pitchers and best hitters while learning to play as a major league shortstop.

Overall, Yount has done pretty well in his short time up in the major leagues. He did make a bunch of errors in '75, and did say that he had some trouble keeping his confidence up. But I think he realizes that when you are just getting started, you will have a few erratic years. He had shown that he knows what to do with the bat and that he has the ability to become a great ballplayer. Most of all, though, the thing Robin has in his favor is a super attitude.

Having a good attitude is really an important part of a player's development. The whole Brewer organization is high on Robin's future, and even that hasn't turned his head. Harvey Kuenn has said that Robin has everything necessary for a career like Al Kaline's, and that's not a bad kind of career to have. Even Hank Aaron has mentioned, more than a couple of times, that Yount has what it takes. To a lesser man, these accolades would have a bad effect on attitude and outlook. That is definitely not the case with our shortstop. If anything, Robin may get down on himself more than he really should.

When he came up to the club, some of the players kidded him a bit about being up so late at night, drinking all of his milk and being sure to get home in time to watch "Sesame Street." But that soon wore off when Robin showed that he could take the heat, and also do a good job in dishing it out. We dress near each other and I have been party to a lot of give and take with him. He has a good sense of humor, and fits in easily with everyone.

He was named the American League's player of the month for April in 1975. At the time, he was still 19, the youngest player to ever receive that honor. But his credentials — a .386 batting average, three home runs, and a slugging percentage of .632 — made him a deserving recipient. In mid-July, he made the cover of "The Sporting News" and many felt he should have been named an alternate to the All-Star team. Barring any serious injuries, Robin Yount should be one of the great shortstops of all time. He has good hands and a good arm, and he swings the bat with discipline. With just a little more experience, he will be an outstanding player.

Besides that, he is well liked by the fans. With all of that blond hair sticking out from under his cap, he has caught the imagination of the older women in the stands, who want to mother him as though he were their own son. And that same head of yellow curls has caught the attention of girls his own age. For them, a chance to talk with him or getting his autograph in their scorebooks is well worth the price of admission to the game. Robin also is a hero to hundreds of kids in the ball parks who entertain the idea of one day being a hot young prospect in the major leagues. Robin takes all of this in stride, presenting himself to the public in the best possible light.

Off the field, Yount is interested in golf, motorcycles and auto racing. He is one of the better golfers, if not the best, on the club. He hasn't played as much recently as he might have normally — he believes that a lot of golf during the season could hinder his batting stroke — but Robin has been able to stay down in the high 70's without much trouble.

His interest in motor sports probably has caused Jim Baumer a few extra gray hairs. It's not unusual for us to see The Kid sitting around reading a motorcycle or racing book when we're on the road. And if we happen to catch him looking at a picture of a guy flying through the air on a dirt bike, or at a bunch of Grand Prix cars taking a very tight turn and ask him if he would like to be in the same spot, his answer is always an excited "Sure!" Back in Woodland Hills, California, Rob has a yellow Porsche and a pretty hot cycle for tooling around town.

On any team with a lot of young players, there are some guys who play most of the time at the expense of other fellows who probably could handle the job. Some guys sit on the bench while others not much older are out on the field. Their only chance of cracking the lineup is an injury to another man or their sometimes dubious promotion to utility status. Often these guys go unnoticed by the fans, even though they turn in a good performance when called upon. We had one of that sort of player on our club in 1975, **Charlie Moore.**

Probably the most underrated ballplayer on the squad, Charlie did a lot to find a place in our lineup. It became obvious to him soon after the season started that the Brewers were going to go with Darrell Porter as the first string catcher, so Charlie looked around, saw our outfield weaknesses, and set about moving from backup catcher to the outfield.

For the last five or six weeks of the season, Moore played some good games out there. He used his head, made the right plays and proved in just a short time that he was a versatile ballplayer who could play effectively at more than one position. A year younger than Porter at 22, Charlie made himself a valuable member of the team.

He still is a fine catcher, and he can play a little infield as well. A former high school football star who turned down a scholarship to Auburn University when he signed with the Brewers, Charlie showed that he could handle himself at the plate by staying in the .290 to .300 range. He probably could play full time with almost any other team as a catcher, or even an outfielder. His first full year with our club was in 1974, so he's still learning the game. But I think it won't be long before he finds himself a permanent position somewhere, if not with the Brewers, with some other major league team.

And then we have a guy who is not only a good relief pitcher, but also the team flake. He does a lot to keep us loose on the bench and ahead of the opposition out on the field. We call him Goofy, but he is better known to the baseball public as **Eddie Rodriguez**.

Pitchers usually are at least a little different from the rest. Some pitchers are hypochondriacs when it comes to their arms, and are constantly trying some treatment or cure for aches, pains or injuries. Talk among pitchers includes charts of how they throw to certain batters, the importance of velocity and humidity on the rotation of the ball, and sometimes even how they can do tricks with balls that have been roughed up, loaded up or have the trade name stamped on in an unusual manner. Pitchers are a breed apart with all of the psyching and fooling around they do on the mound, and Eddie just may be one of the most different of all.

A native of Puerto Rico, our resident jester is

always laughing and cracking jokes in the locker room or on the bench. You may just be sitting in the dugout, waiting for the game to start, and he'll walk by, say something funny in his own Spanish-English way, and the whole team breaks up. Or, you may be stretching your arm to straighten your undershirt. If Ed sees what you're doing, he'll do the same thing. And if you ask how he's feeling, but do it with your neck sort of turned around in an unusual way, darned if he won't do the very same thing and say that he's just fine.

We had a lot of fun with him during the Friday afternoon kangaroo court sessions. Every once in a while someone would charge Eddie with eating in the locker room before the game, or talking with guys on the other team. He would tell his side of the story, but because he is hard to understand, the judges would ask him to repeat it two or three times. Eddie would say his piece once or twice and then get mad at the court, mumble something, and pay his one or two dollar fine. Sometimes we never found out what he had said.

When he gets out on that pitcher's mound, though, Rodriguez is all business. Just 23, he has been one of the most effective relief pitchers on the club. Even with a sore shoulder for a portion of 1975, Eddie had a 7-0 record.

He played volleyball and baseball in high school, and likes to swim and go to the movies. He also enjoys playing the lottery in Puerto Rico. He almost won

$100,000 in the off-season one year. Of course, almost winning a lottery is like almost hitting a home run. It's nice to speculate on, but you don't get anything out of it. There was one particular series of numbers Eddie played each week, but for some reason he failed to make his play on the week that his series finally paid off. Maybe it's better that he didn't win all that money. If he had, there's no doubt in my mind that he would have shown up for spring training sometime in late March, only after he had spent all of his winnings.

Tom Murphy, another relief pitcher, is just the opposite. He's almost all business. Murph joined the club in December of 1973, when infielder Bobbie Heise was sent to the Cardinals, and that deal has proved to be a steal for us. Tom had a super year in '74, recording 20 saves and 10 victories while posting an earned run average of 1.90. He had to fight off the effects of a sore shoulder for part of the '75 season but he brought home another 20 saves. He appeared to have regained his old stuff in his last five or six outings of the season and proved, I think, that his great '74 performances were not flukes.

One of the half-dozen or so men on the roster who has either finished his college education or is continuing it during the off-season, Tom holds a bachelor of arts degree in English and history from the University of Ohio. I think we're going to be seeing more and more players coming to the big leagues with college backgrounds. Many of the young guys signing these days have it in their contracts that the club must pay for the completion of their education. Ballplayers are looking more to the future, and many of them feel that they will be able to combine careers in the big leagues and the academic world.

Murphy has had experience as a short relief man, a starter and a long reliever. Changes in assignments can make it hard for a guy to know just where he fits in best, but I think Tom has found that he can do the job best just going two or three innings every couple of days. The short reliever has to have a different outlook on the game than the guys in the regular rotation. Murphy has come to like his role as a short man, and he enjoys warming up almost every game out in the bull pen. His philosophy seems to be that the more you throw the ball, the better it is for you.

Talking about pitchers on our staff, the man I think could have been our best in 1975 was **Pete Broberg**. Pete came to us in the deal that sent Clyde Wright to the Texas Rangers. Before becoming a Brewer, he had never won more than five or six games in any one of his big league seasons. But in his first year with us, he had a 14-16 record and showed what he is made of by re-earning a place in the starting rotation after having lost it.

Broberg started the year fast, and his record in the middle of May was 6-3. But something happened to him in his next several appearances that Del and pitching coach Ken McBride didn't like. His record slid to 10-10 and they removed him from the starting rotation and worked on his delivery. They thought Pete was wasting a lot of motion in his wind-up, so they converted him to the no-windup style.

Pete worked on it, gave a couple of good performances in relief, and soon was back to starting status. He throws the ball well, has shown a lot of determination in getting his program back together, and should be a guy we can count on for some time to come.

Another of our college boys, Broberg went to Dartmouth College after high school, turning down a reported $175,000 offer from Oakland to turn pro. After a great career at the Ivy League school, Pete signed with the Washington Senators for about $150,000 in 1971.

Pitchers sometimes have a harder time getting used to major league play than other players, especially when they have had little or no prior professional experience. Pete's trips back to the minors early in his career show that he might have had a little control problem and that he needed a less pressured atmosphere to really learn his job. From what he showed us his first year on the club, I'd say that he has learned his lessons real well.

Another trade — this one in May of '75 — turned out to be a good one for us, too. Outfielder **Bill Sharp** came to our club from the White Sox in exchange for Bob Coluccio. We wanted another left handed batter on the roster, but we also got a pretty fair outfielder in the bargain.

Billy was able to step in when needed and turned out to be one of our top defensive outfielders. A player of compact build — he played football at Ohio State — Sharp was usually put into the game in the late innings for defensive purposes. He could be counted on to get his share of extra base hits, and I found him to be a great clutch ballplayer.

It would be hard for me to talk about the inner workings and personalities of the Milwaukee Brewers and not include something about **Del Crandall**.

Del began playing pro ball in 1947 in Leavenworth, Kansas and moved through the minor leagues until he got his chance to catch for the Boston Braves in 1949. From then through 1963 — with the exception of two years out for military service — Del was the Braves' man behind the plate in both Boston and Milwaukee. He went to the San Francisco Giants as part of a multi-player deal in 1964, spent one year in the Bay Area, was traded to the Pirates in 1965, got his release at the end of that season and finished his playing career in the majors with the Cleveland Indians in 1966.

Five times a National League All-Star, Del played in both the 1957 and 1958 World Series. He led the league in starting double plays as a catcher twice, and tied a National League record for being the top receiver in assists a total of six times. Crandall also tied a World Series record in 1957 for starting two double plays, and was named the Gold Glove catcher in the National League in 1958, '59, '60 and '62. In 1,573 big league games, Del scored 585 runs, got 1,276 hits, 179 home runs and had a lifetime batting average of .254.

Del spent two years out of baseball, then began his managerial career with the Dodgers' Albuquerque club of the Texas League in 1969. In 1971, he took over the Brewers' Evansville operation and stayed with that team until May 29, 1972, when he was named to take over the big club after Dave Bristol was fired.

I think our club is rough on a manager because we have so many young ballplayers. When you have a young club, the players have to be treated differently from those on a veteran team, with the younger players just waiting for a chance. When a club has lots of veterans, there's not much to worry about when a tight situation comes up. Most of the guys will know how to handle it. But with so many youngsters, it's different.

If the manager chews out a younger player, the player may think he is being picked on, when really all that is happening is an effort to get him to realize what he has done and how to correct the problem. That's one problem we have had on our club — trying to get the young guys to stay with the game and not give up or take the attitude that they're in the doghouse.

Del knows what makes good baseball, but I won't say he didn't make any mistakes. All managers make them. The manager's primary job is to see that his players give 100% all the time. That's really all you can ask of the man. He can only work with the players he has, and, if the lineup turns out to be a winner, the manager is a great guy and all that. But, if the men he puts on the field don't do the job, he probably gets more than his share of the blame. Building confidence, getting the guys to put out all of the time and keeping things on an even keel is really just about all a manager can do. But as most of the 24 men in that position will tell you, it's not the easiest thing in the world.

I thought Del did a pretty good job with the Brewers. There were times when some of the players lost their respect for him and made his job, and our job as a team, harder. I don't think that all of the fault was in the way Del handled the club, either. Professional ballplayers acting in an unprofessional manner accounted for some of the trouble. And, in those cases, much of Del's effectiveness was hampered.

Personally, I think Del Crandall is a super guy. I never had any trouble going in to talk to him about anything, and I give Del a lot of credit for my still playing ball in the big leagues. When I joined the club for the 1973 season, I was coming off a couple of not-so-good years with the Phillies. I was hitting only .180 or .185 in the third month of the season, and with two bad years behind me, it would have been easy for Del to sit me down on the bench and let another guy have a chance to play as a regular. I might have gotten into the wrong frame of mind and never come out of the predicament I found myself in. But Del hung in there with me and I hope I rewarded him at least a little by putting together three pretty good years while he was the boss.

Del and Henry Aaron are more than pretty good friends. They had a special kind of respect and admiration for one another. Aaron tried to help some of the younger players along, but only to give Del a hand, not to circumvent Del's authority. I think they'll be great friends for many years to come.

Chapter 10

Hank's Highlights

Henry Aaron's baseball career goes back to his early youth in Mobile, Alabama, where he was born February 5, 1934. There is nothing unusual about a young fellow's interest in baseball, but there is something at least slightly different about Hank's development. By the time he was a high school junior, he was playing the game for more than just fun. He joined the semipro Mobile Bears, earning a little extra money for the family.

After graduation, there was no question that Aaron wanted to make a career of baseball. He joined the Indianapolis Clowns of the old Negro American League — a league that eventually died out with the acceptance of blacks in the major leagues — for

$200 a month. He was unschooled in the refinements of baseball but he made up for that lack in sheer talent. He batted crosshanded, but with his quick, strong wrists still led the league in hitting with a .467 mark. That was enough to convince Braves' scout Dewey Griggs that Hank had untapped potential. The Braves signed Aaron as an infielder, then assigned him to their farm club at Eau Claire, Wisconsin, where in just two weeks he was impressive enough to be voted to the All-Star team in the Class D Northern League. He finished the 1952 season as rookie of the year in that league with a .336 batting average.

That earned him a promotion to Jacksonville of the Class A Sally League. He was switched from shortstop to second base at Jacksonville, but continued pounding the ball. In 1953, at 19, he led the league in runs scored with 115, hits with 208, doubles with 36, RBI's with 125, and batting average with .362. He had shown enough. He joined the Braves for spring training in 1954.

The Braves had a veteran infield at the start of the 1954 training camp, and Aaron didn't figure to crack it, so he was shifted to the outfield. He wasn't expected to earn starting status there, either, but the newly acquired Bobby Thomson suffered a broken ankle during an early exhibition game against the New York Yankees, and suddenly there was an open berth in the outfield. Aaron moved in, and was never moved out. He hit a respectable .280 in 122 games his first year. Ironically, that season was cut short for him when he, too, suffered a broken ankle in an early September doubleheader against the Reds at Cincinnati. That particular day, before the injury, was an impressive one, though. He had five straight hits. And that particular season was the start of something big. In his next 11, he hit under .300 only once, in 1960, when he finished at .292.

Over the years, Hank led the National League in a number of offensive categories. In 1957, '66 and '69, he was the home run champion, and he tied for the title in 1963. He was tops in slugging percentage (doubles, triples and home runs) in 1959, '63 and '67, and in 1971 he led the league with a career high of .669. He was the National League leader in total bases for eight of the 14 seasons from 1956 through 1967, and first in RBI's in 1957, '60, '63 and '66.

As an outfielder, Aaron was the leader in starting double plays in 1960, '64 and '66; won Gold Gloves for fielding in 1958, '59 and '60; and was named player of the year in 1956 and 1963 by The Sporting News. He hit three home runs in the 1969 pennant playoff with the New York Mets, has hit three homers in World Series play and two in All-Star competition. None of those count among his record 745 homers. And on June 8, 1961, against the Reds' Eddie Mathews, Aaron, Joe Adcock and Frank Thomas hit consecutive home runs, setting a major league record.

Hank was the National League's Most Valuable

Player in 1957, and is one of only five players to hit 30 home runs and steal 30 bases in one season — 44 homers and 31 steals in 1963. He also has hit three home runs in a single home game, June 21, 1959. He was the 1970 recipient of the Lou Gehrig Award, given the major leaguer who best exemplifies the character and courage of the former Yankee first baseman.

Henry Aaron also holds more than 20 major league records, among which are these:

Most home runs — 745

Most games — 3,213

Most at bats — 12,093

Most consecutive seasons 100 games
    or more — 22

Most long hits — 1,459

Most total bases — 6,756

Most seasons 20 or more home runs — 20

Most sacrifice flies — 119

Most RBI's — 2,262

Most seasons 100 or more games — 22

Most years 100 or more runs scored — 15

Most years 30 or more home runs — 15

And then there are the National League records Hank earned from 1954 through 1974:

Most runs scored — 2,107

Most home runs, bases loaded — 16

Most home runs, outfielder — 661

Most consecutive batting streaks of 20 or more games a season — 4

Most home runs by a right handed hitter — 733

Most years 40 or more home runs — 8

Most years leading league in total bases — 8

Most years 300 or more total bases — 15

In addition, he also has accounted for the following records:

Hits in career — 3,709
    (2nd only to Ty Cobb)

Runs scored — 2,152

Doubles — 616

Triples — 98

Stolen bases —240

Lifetime average through 1975 — .3067

A Rundown of Hank Aaron's Milestone Home Runs

No.	Date	Opponent	Pitcher	Remarks
1	4/23/54	@ St. Louis	Vic Raschi	1st N. L. homer
100	8/15/57	@ Cincinnati	Don Gross	100th N. L. homer
109	9/23/57	St. Louis	Billy Muffet	Won '57 pennant
200	7/ 3/60	@ St. Louis	Ron Kline	200th N. L. homer
300	4/19/63	@ New York	Roger Craig	300th N. L. homer
400	4/20/66	@ Philadelphia	Bo Belinsky	400th N. L. homer
500	7/14/68	San Francisco	Mike McCormick	500th N. L. homer
600	4/27/71	San Francisco	Gaylord Perry	600th N. L. homer
661	8/ 6/72	@ Cincinnati	Don Gullett	moved into second spot on all-time list

700	7/21/73	Philadelphia	Ken Brett	700th N. L. homer
714	4/ 4/74	@ Cincinnati	Jack Billingham	tied Babe Ruth
715	4/ 8/74	Los Angeles	Al Downing	became all-time leader
734	4/18/75	@ Cleveland	Gaylord Perry	1st A. L. homer
745	9/14/75	@ Boston	Bill Lee	12th and last of season

Appendix

About
Don Money

There is a television commercial that pops up every now and again showing men who would rather drive a pickup truck than a car. Most notable of these are baseball's Catfish Hunter and the grand old man of the National Football League, George Blanda. It would not, however, be out of line to add Don Money's name to that list.

Although his white pickup is of a different make than those in the TV spot, it is the vehicle Don finds himself most comfortable in during the off-season. The family sedan — a modest two door black model — generally is reserved for Sharon Money's trips to the store. Flashy transportation just doesn't fit in with Don Money's lifestyle.

If the Brewers' third baseman had played in Dizzy Dean's era, he could rightly have been described as a "down-home country boy." He likes people and people like him.

Not only can he play the game, he also relates well to the people who pay to see him and his teammates perform. Don is aware of his responsibilities to the fans, and relays that feeling to those who seek his attention. When signing his autograph, Money takes care that the signature is just as clear and legible as the one he signs on the back of his paycheck.

As a player, he is good — darn good! Del Crandall once said of Money that his value stems from his ability to do so many things so well. It's true. He can run, throw, hit and field. He also can wiggle his ears! Other ballplayers and front office people alike respect his baseball knowledge. He could be a valuable baseball executive when his playing career is over.

There is, however, more to his baseball personality than just knowledge and skill. There is a lot inside the man that places him a mark or two above most.

A quiet leader, Money is a veteran player whose first responsibilities are directly related to the betterment of his team. Like all professional athletes, Don likes to win and he goes all out with that effort in mind. On the baseball diamond, on the racquetball court or at the kitchen table for a card game, he wants to come out on top. But his attitude toward winning on the baseball field is different from the one he exhibits as he tallies a winning score after a hand of gin rummy. On the field, it's hustle, hustle, hustle. But when the game is for fun, he plays to win, but he plays to have a good time, too.

During the baseball season, Don's work clothes are the Brewers' doubleknit uniforms. But from October to March, his attire is the best set of permanent press work twills Sears has to offer. If he had his druthers, those gray and green outfits would be all he would ever wear. There is lots of work for him to do on his little 2½ acre farm, and he loves it.

The work is hard, but by its very nature is relaxing to him, since it is such a change from the traveling and ballplaying that keep him away from home so much of the time.

Raising cattle and chickens, remodeling sheds and repairing fences all seem to keep Don Money in good spirits and go right along with the country boy image. Country boy, yes. Hayseed, no. Although his formal education ended with his graduation from high school in LaPlata, Maryland, he has not let his professional baseball career stop his personal growth and development in other fields. His regular reading material includes, but is not limited to, The Sporting News, many of the popular news magazines, daily newspapers and an occasional glance at The Wall Street Journal to see how his few shares of stock are doing. He enjoys history, crossword puzzles, documentaries on TV, adventure and science fiction movies, and a quiet hour or two in front of the fireplace in his recently completed den. He loves spaghetti, will have an occasional beer and can think of no better dinner than a steak or roast from one of the animals in his herd of beef cattle.

A comparative newcomer to radio sports broadcasting, Don likes the immediacy of play-by-play work. Candid in his commentary, he is not afraid to make a mistake on the air, nor too proud to apologize for it.

Although humor is a part of his life, it's not the kind that jumps out at you. When he jokes, the joke is often on him. When speaking at banquets, he usually talks on subjects that relate to his experiences in the sports world, and he fields questions with all the skill he shows at third base. He is bright, subtle and interested in many things. There is surely much more to him than what the box score shows.

Don Money is a warm and close friend whose friendship is valued because of the kind of man he is, not because he is a ballplayer. Working with him on this book allowed me to know him a little better. For that alone, I'm glad he asked me to help.

— HERB ANASTOR

The Aaron
I Remember

Have you ever seen Henry Aaron play? "Live" or on television? Chances are that you have, and that's one of the reasons this book appealed to you. In the course of his 22-year career, Aaron must have been seen by over 50 million fans — "live" — and conceivably a billion or more via television. This makes him a unique legend; certainly the first of the electronic era.

As the author, his editors and the publisher worked on preparing this volume for printing, it became evident that a unique and valuable opportunity existed for every reader. How exciting it would be to be able to take a volume on Ty Cobb, Connie Mack, Lou Gehrig or Babe Ruth from the family library or bookshelf and find in it a record of the times grandpa saw them play. How he felt as new records were made, and to have him share with us his reactions to the radio broadcasts of the 1928 World Series and Ruth's record-setting performance! This is your chance to write your own chapter in this salute to Henry Aaron — to record for your own family how you felt when Henry led all batters in the 1957 World Series, when he established a new home run record.

And even if you've only seen him play on television's "Game of the Week," you'll find *your* chapter a valuable and fun reminiscence in years to come. The pages which follow contain a few questions to aid your own recollection.

When did I first see Henry Aaron play?

The date:

The location:

His team:

Opponent:

What I remember about the day and Aaron's performance in the field and at bat.

Did you ever meet Aaron or get his autograph?

Did you ever see him hit a home run?

If you are over 25, what was your reaction when you saw, heard, or learned about Aaron's 11th inning home run which brought Milwaukee its first pennant in 1957?

216

When did you first become aware he had an opportunity to establish a new all-time home run record?
How did you feel at the time?

Where were you when Hank hit the home run which placed him in first place as new Home Run King? What did you say to family and friends at the time?

218

How did you feel when you learned Aaron would complete his career as a Milwaukee Brewer?

If you have seen him play "live" as a Brave *and* as a Brewer, what does that experience mean to you?

On these pages, record for your family and heirs to come, all that you would like to share with them about your memory of Henry Aaron (recollections not covered on previous pages).

Date:

Place:

Your Name: